THE FINANCING OF SHIP ACQUISITIONS

by Frank Paine

Fairplay Publications

Published and distributed by
FAIRPLAY PUBLICATIONS LTD.
20 Ullswater Crescent,
Ullswater Business Park,
Coulsdon, Surrey CR5 2HR
Telephone: 081-660 2811
Fax: 081-660 2824
Telex: 884595 FRPLAY G

ISBN 0 905045 955

First Published January 1989
Reprinted November 1990

Produced by SB Datagraphics Ltd., Colchester, for Fairplay Publications

The Author

Frank Paine graduated from Stanford University in 1968 with an AB degree in Political Science. Following a stint of almost four years in the U.S. Army as a Portuguese translator, he joined the Hartford National Bank (now the Connecticut National Bank) as a Credit Analyst. He spent the next approximately four years in that capacity, advancing to Senior Credit Analyst, and simultaneously studying for a Masters Degree in Business Administration. He completed this degree at the head of his class in 1976.

Thereafter, he joined the Bankers Trust Company to assist with credit decisions for the International Banking Department, which at that time included the Shipping Division. Two years later, he joined the Shipping Division, where he broke new ground by initiating the bank's programs for calling on shipowners in Canada and Latin America.

In 1982, he joined the New York branch of the Algemene Bank Nederland to found and manage its ship financing division. He subsequently left to found F. Paine & Associates Inc., a firm providing financial consulting services to new ventures, principally in the shipping industry. From 1986–1990 he was the chief credit officer for North America of the Saudi International Bank (an affiliate of the Morgan Guaranty Trust Company), and oversaw all of the Bank's exposure to the shipping industry. Since resigning therefrom, he has been pursuing other business opportunities related to shipping and ship finance.

Mr. Paine is married, and lives with his wife and two golden retrievers in Stamford, Connecticut. In addition to his work, he enjoys classical music, drama, and running.

Acknowledgements

As I complete this book, I wish to acknowledge certain intellectual debts to various people who, whether they realize it or not, contributed to the background I bring to bear on the subject.

In particular, I am grateful to Guy Huntley, who made it possible for me to learn the techniques of financial analysis; to Chris Lloyd, from whom I learned the basic principles of ship finance; to John Lang, from whom I learned some of the more esoteric aspects of ship mortgages; to Derick Betts, who in addition to helping me incorporate my company, educated me about certain important taxation concepts; and to Carl Samuelson, who introduced me to the net working investment concept.

I am also grateful to Fairplay Publications for being so patient with a project that has taken considerably longer than originally expected, and to my wife, Frederica, for her sage advice, encouragement, and assistance with graphics.

It goes without saying that any errors and/or omissions are solely my responsibility.

Table of Contents

Preface to Second Printing of The Financing of Ship Aquisitions

Since the first printing of *The Financing of Ship Acquisitions* a number of things have changed. As predicted, the cycle did change, mostly for the better. There are signs that the dry cargo market may have gone full circle, with freight rates again dropping down into four figures/day for a Panamax bulkcarrier (in fact, rates never did recover to the level necessary to repay the debt on a newbuilding). While turmoil in the Middle East has made the tanker market drop off, at least for now observers have become increasingly conscious of the fact that over the next five to ten years, a major portion of the world tanker fleet will have to be replaced, and that with newbuilding prices at unprecedented levels, the capital requirements will be at a level never seen before. While present rates would not justify a newbuilding order, it is expectations of future rates that will govern orders, and it seems inevitable that rates will at some point move a long way towards closing the present gap. The principal question is timing, which is subject to a great deal of heated debate. In addition to the Middle East turmoil, such issues as the opening of Eastern Europe, pollution liability retrofitting, and double hulls will all have some impact.

Despite these uncertainties, financial institutions have begun to notice this underlying factor in the tanker market. Some, which have a history of involvement in ship finance, have been rebuilding their ship finance departments, and have been distressed to find that much expertise has been lost. Others, with no such history are taking the proverbial leap using people whose experience can only be described (and that generously) as thin. In short, I have been pleased to see that several of the major premises that gave rise to the book in the first place have been proven to be correct. I only hope that it may play a small part in preventing repetition of some of the mistakes of the past.

In reviewing the text in preparation for the second printing, I have only detected one significant error of fact. First International Capital Corporation (FICC), which now has its headquarters in Naples, Florida, is understood to be wholly owned by a company controlled by Mr Paul Slater. Henry Ansbacher is understood to no longer have any interest in FICC. The press recently reported FICC's recent investment in a joint venture with the Wescol Group to provide leasing and ship management services. It seems likely that it will be a significant player in that business.

With respect to financial intermediaries, there are at least two new participants in the market. One of these is Marine Equity Corporation, a New York based partnership of Mr Milton Kliger, formerly Chief Financial

Officer of the Overseas Shipholding Group, and Mr Robert DiMarsico, formerly of the Marine Midland Bank. The other is Vita Marine Financial Services Limited, which is backed by two well known maritime companies, V Ships (the Vlasov Group of Monte Carlo), and ABC Maritime, and headed by Mr Arnoult Gauthier, formerly of Credit Commercial de France. It is premature to project any particular strategic direction for either of these two ventures.

Chapter One

Introduction

The severe depression in the shipping markets for the last five years has left its mark on both owners and financiers of marine transportation equipment. As one talks to the institutions that have traditionally financed this sector, one cannot help but be struck by the number that for the time being are for practical purposes totally unable to consider new business. Some have ship financing specialists that must spend literally all of their working hours handling workout situations.[1] Once these situations have been cleaned up as best they can, it is difficult to say under what conditions new business may be considered, if at all. Other institutions have taken the more radical step of discontinuing their ship financing departments, and either reassigning or laying off their ship financing specialists. The workout situations have been turned over to specialized workout departments.

No market stays depressed forever, and this paralysis at most of the ship financing institutions is part of the process of supply/demand readjustment in the shipping markets. There will come a time when financial institutions will once again find ship financing attractive because the supply/demand readjustment will swing the other direction, resulting in rates of return that justify the risks (if these are properly understood). In fact, recent developments particularly in the tanker market suggest that their renewal of interest may not be far off.

However, when this happens, many of the institutions will no longer have staffs that can properly analyze the risks and competently document the transactions. Insofar as the prevalence of workout situations at some institutions has been attributable to bad judgement or fraud, the lack of availability of such people is no loss. On the other hand, the relative lack of good people makes it highly likely that the mistakes of the past will be repeated.

One of the reasons for writing this book, therefore, is to provide a basis fo training people, and hopefully avoiding at least some of these mistakes However, there is another reason as well.

Inevitably, borrowers and lenders in general have somewhat differen perspectives. This is true "in spades" when it comes to shipowners and shi financiers. The shipowner wishes to conserve his capital, investing as littl of it as possible so as to maximize the return. The ship financier, on the othe hand, wants the shipowner to invest as much of his own capital as possibl so as to reduce the financial risk.

By the same token, the shipowner and the ship financier often have differin perceptions of risk. In a weak market, the owner may well resist fixing hi vessels on a period basis because that could mean missing a possible uptur in the market. His point of view is not necessarily invalid. The financia institution, on the other hand, having no taste for market risk, may well insis that the financed vessels be fixed on a period basis. Such a fixture gives a least the illusion and sometimes the reality of eliminating market risk although the reality seems to be becoming increasingly rare.

Clearly, this is a communications issue. There is a special case of the communications problem that is also worthy of note. This has to do with the fleet development aspirations of developing countries. Even when most developing or semi-industrialized countries had ready access to the international financial markets, their private sector shipowners (with only a few exceptions) generally did not (for the purposes of this argument, one can reasonably ignore flags of convenience such as Liberia and Panama, as the owners in question are almost always non-residents).

It is very difficult to establish an economically viable private shipowning sector without the owners having direct access to the international financial markets. The present generalized debt service problems of many of the developing and semi-industrialized countries will in many cases and at some point subside to the extent that they will gradually once again have access to the international financial markets. As capital becomes increasingly available, many of these countries, having sharply reduced their investment in the capital intensive shipowning industry in order to conserve their resources, will in all likelihood renew their interest in acquiring ships. However, unless certain things happen their private shipowning sectors will still not, as a rule, have the direct access to the international financial markets that they require.

One alternative, of course, is to arrange such access under the umbrellas of either the governments involved, or internationally respected commercial banks. Where this has been tried to any great degree, as for instance in Brazil, the results in terms of long term economic viability and eventual financial independence have left a great deal to be desired.

Provided the shipowners in these countries are able to arrange for certain changes in their operating and legal environments, and provided they take certain strategic measures, there is no reason why they cannot, over time gain access to the international financial markets. Indeed, if the financial institutions properly understand the issues, there are situations in these countries that are or will become bankable sooner than the country in general, and thus represent some very interesting opportunities.

Thus, in addition to attempting to make a small contribution to the training of the next generation of ship financing officers, this book will seek to close two important communications gaps: that between shipowner and ship financier, and that between shipowners in developing countries and international financial institutions. Though the book will consider the perspectives of both shipowner and ship financier, it is a book about ship financing rather than about the financial analysis of investments in shipping. It will thus of necessity emphasize the financier's point of view, though the understanding of this point of view is hardly irrelevant to the shipowner. Indeed, there are sections that will seem excessively familiar to most commercial banking officers: they have been included primarily for the benefit of the owner.

The author's qualifications for writing on the subject of ship finance include sixteen years of involvement in international finance. Almost half of this time was spent in arranging finance for shipowners: first, as a commercial banking officer at one of New York's money center banks (among other things, he was the first ship finance officer in that bank to call on Latin American shipowners); second, as Vice President in charge of ship finance for the U.S. operations of a major European bank; and last, as President of F. Paine & Associates, Inc., a consulting firm/merchant banking firm specializing in ship finance. To the best of the author's knowledge, no financial institution has ever incurred any loss whatsoever as a result of any ship financing relationship he has ever developed or (in the case of the merchant banking business) offered.

It is worth noting that though the emphasis in this book will be on the financing of ship purchases, most of the same principles apply to the finance of equipment for employment in offshore oil exploration and development: drilling rigs, production platforms, supply and support vessels, diving vessels, and so forth. The key is whether the equipment is defined in law as a marine vessel(s), and in most jurisdictions, this kind of equipment is so defined.

The next two chapters of the book will focus on sources of ship finance for new construction, and the domination in this area of various official export credit programs (Chapter II); and for vessel purchases in the second-hand market, and the domination in this area of commercial banks, using a variation of project finance, but usually with recourse to the owner (Chapter III). Chapter IV will be a discussion of the financing of U.S. flag vessels, which is a very special case, and Chapter V will be a discussion of the declining business of vessel leasing and bareboat chartering. Chapter VI will be a discussion of the various types of ship financing institutions and intermediaries.

Chapter VII will focus on the analysis of the ship financing transaction. It is broken into three major sectors (bulk shipping, liner shipping, and vessel operating pools), each of which involves a fundamentally different set of analytical concepts. The chapter finishes with a section on the not generally well understood subject of country risk as it pertains to ship finance.

Chapter VIII will assume that the terms of a ship financing transaction have been agreed and will focus on the documentation of the transaction. Here the author will argue that while it is tempting to leave this area to the discretion of attorneys, there are many aspects of the documents that both the owner and financier should be aware of, as they will have a direct bearing on the future course of the relationship. Indeed, poor documentation can make it inevitable from the beginning that a workout situation will develop, whereas good documentation can forestall many a workout situation, or at the very least, mitigate the losses if a workout situation does develop.

Chapter IX will focus on the special problems (and opportunities) related to ship financing for owners in developing countries. It will address the requirements of the international ship financing community, and make some suggestions for meeting those requirements.

Chapter X will be a brief discussion of workout situations. It implicitly acknowledges that such situations will inevitably arise from time to time, and offers some thoughts for both owners and financiers as to why these situations are to be avoided if at all possible; what financiers can expect to encounter if they are forced to arrest a vessel; and how owners experiencing difficulties may consider behaving.

Notes

1. Workout situation refers to a situation in which the borrower is unable to repay the loan and it becomes necessary to restructure or work out another means of payment.

Chapter Two

Finance for New Construction: The Domination of Official Export Credits

Shipping by sea continues to provide the lowest unit transportation cost. As it is the principal form of transportation in international trade, it is by definition international in scope.

With respect to new construction ("newbuildings") the choice of the building country rests within certain outside limits imposed by construction quality and technological sophistication, on price attractiveness. Price attractiveness is in some cases a function of a comparative advantage in labor costs, as in China and Korea. Alternatively, where shipyards are major employers, the labor intensive nature of the business results in abnormal political sensitivity to the level of contract work in the shipyards, in turn resulting in the availability of price subsidies. In Brazil and Germany, for instance, such subsidies often amount to 30-50% of the actual cost. Lastly, shipbuilding contracts usually include financing on attractive terms (particularly in a high interest rate environment) through official export credit agencies. The Japanese and Korean programs are the best known, but there are also attractive programs in the U.K., Greece, Singapore, Spain, Brazil, France, and Belgium. Denmark has a program that appears to be unique. Lastly, some countries have special financing programs for buyers in developing or semi-industrialized countries.

In as capital intensive a business as ship ownership, it comes as no great surprise that financing terms can make or break any given transaction. Given the labor intensive nature of ship construction, and hence the political sensitivity of ship exports, it also comes as no great surprise that the financing of new construction is heavily dominated by official export credit agencies.

There are basically three types of export credit programs. Most involve direct finance from the local export financing agency to the buyer of the vessel, but in some cases the credit takes the form of notes issued by the buyer to the shipyard under the construction contract. The shipyard then sells the notes to the export credit agency, or borrows against them. From time to time, some of the export credit agencies package a group of export credits, and sell them on a discounted basis, with or without recourse, to syndicates of international commercial banks. The Export-Import Bank of Korea (KEXIM) has done this several times over the years, and a similar non-recourse package was once done on behalf of Brazil's CACEX.

However, a few of the programs are done on an interest subsidy basis, under which an official export credit agency merely guarantees to commercial banks actually providing finance that their yield on the transaction will be at least some specified spread over LIBOR (London Interbank Offered Rate), even though the rate to the borrower is fixed at 7-9%. In other words, the export credit agency makes up the difference, but takes no credit risk, and is not responsible for providing any funding. The U.K., Brazil, Greece and Singapore all have programs of this type available.

A few export credit programs are based on government guarantees of commercial bank finance, but these are comparatively rare in ship finance.

The terms of the official export credits are in most cases some variation on the terms agreed upon a few years ago by the OECD[1] member nations: amount, 80% of contract price; tenor or term, 8 years; interest rate, 9% fixed; and amortization, equal semi-annual installments of principal. There are, however, some notable variations with respect to the security[2] required and the currency of the financing.

For instance, the Export-Import Bank of Japan requires as security for the credit a first mortgage over the vessel, but also requires in the absence of a time charter, that the first seven installments be covered by a bank guarantee or standby letter of credit (the standby letter of credit[3] is peculiar to U.S. banks, which are prohibited by law from issuing guarantees). This creates a technical problem, as the bank issuing the guarantee must rely for security on a second mortgage, which is not very attractive, as the bank can take no action unless permitted to by the holder of the first mortgage. In most cases, the bank issuing the guarantee requires additional security from the shipowner's other assets. The Japanese Eximbank has been known to forego the guarantee in cases involving an unusually low finance ratio.[4]

Another difficulty with the Japanese export credit is that it is available only in yen. Since most ocean freight is payable in U.S. dollars, the borrower under this program must assume a major foreign exchange risk, which is very expensive (though not impossible) to hedge for its full term. An export credit denominated in a strengthening yen may add greatly to the cost of the vessel.

Because of these two difficulties, as well as the perception that the gap between Euro-yen interest rates and the fixed rate quoted by the Export-Import Bank of Japan is not very great, more and more shipowners are turning to commercial banks to finance new construction in Japan. In fact, until relatively recently much of the slack created by the non-competitive official export credit program was taken up by Japanese banks, which were both willing and able to extend the tenor to ten or more years; make U.S. dollar loans; provide exchange risk guarantees; and/or arrange long-term Japanese tax leases, which represented 100% financing.

In contrast to the Japanese program, KEXIM makes credits available in U.S. dollars, thus doing away with the foreign exchange risk. However, KEXIM prefers to take no credit risk at all, and thus requires that the entire financing be covered by a bank guarantee or standby letter of credit. This makes the first mortgage available to the bank issuing the guarantee, which may also provide a "wrap around" facility to extend the term to ten or more years, with one or two years grace with respect to principal payments. When a new construction order is particularly attractive, KEXIM has been known to grant concessionary terms. For instance when United States Lines ordered a series of twelve new container ships a few years ago (total value approximately $750 million), KEXIM provided ten year financing.

The Spanish export credit is made available in either U.S. dollars or pesetas, and requires as security a revolving bank guarantee/standby letter of credit equal to three principal installments as well as the first mortgage.

In contrast to all of these, the Brazilian CACEX, Banque Française de Commerce Exterieure (BFCE) and the British Export Credit Guarantee Department (ECGD) are all willing to take the full credit risk, relying solely on the first mortgage for security. However, the Brazilian credit is available only in U.S. dollars, whereas the French and British credits are available in either U.S. dollars or local currency.

In an effort to generate additional sea going employment as well as shipyard jobs, the Belgian government has established a program providing significant financial benefits to shipowners that not only contract new construction in Belgium, but also agree to place all or a portion of their vessels under the Belgian flag. Owners agreeing to this scheme, such as the Montreal based

Fednav Group, have been able to obtain fifteen year credit terms, at 1% interest, with an exchange rate guarantee. These benefits are at least partly offset by the abnormally high contract prices and Belgian flag operating costs, but have nevertheless been found attractive by certain shipowners preferring not to operate under a flag of convenience.[5]

Denmark has a program usually referred to as the ''Danish bond program''. The workings of this unique program are very complex, but a perhaps oversimplified conceptual description is as follows: upon placing a newbuilding order in a Danish shipyard, the buyer arranges a (usually) U.S. dollar bank borrowing for some percentage of the contract price. The proceeds are placed in a trust under the management of a Danish bank, together with the proceeds of certain subsidies and an official credit facility. The trust is then invested in long term Danish government bonds, and is assigned to the shipyard in full payment of the construction contract (i.e., both equity and official credit). The trust, together with the interest earned on the bonds, is sufficient to fully cover these obligations. Upon delivery of the vessel, the shipowner's only remaining obligation is for the U.S. dollar loan, resulting effectively in 100% financing, and an up to 40% reduction in the purchase price of the ship.

This program, on the surface, sounds almost too good to be true. There are in fact pre-conditions that make it attractive only in very limited circumstances. It is actually an early form of defeasance, relying upon interest rate differentials between U.S. dollars and Danish kroner, in a rather imaginative structure, to achieve a favorable economic result. However, though Danish built vessels have an excellent reputation for quality, they tend to be relatively expensive. Therefore, no shipowner should seriously consider ordering one under the bond program, without examining all details and preconditions. The best source for this purpose would probably be an internationally oriented Danish bank maintaining foreign offices: Privatbanken A/S for instance.

Some countries make available unusually attractive credit terms for ship purchasers from developing or semi-industrialized countries. These programs vary greatly from each other and over time, so that any attempt to cover them here would be more misleading than useful. Just to give the general flavor of this sort of thing, however, Norway either has or used to have a program, limited to buyers from developing countries, providing for up to 80% financing on the security of a first priority mortgage, but with no principal repayments in the first three years. This was intended to allow the buyer to borrow the remaining 20% (i.e. achieve 100% financing) on the security of a second mortgage, but with repayment during the three year grace period. While there is no guarantee that this (or any similar) program will be available in a country in which the buyer wishes to order a ship, the possibility should not be overlooked.

The foregoing discussion of official export credit programs is not intended to be exhaustive. Other countries build ships, and most countries that build ships, make official export credit available. For example, the Republic of China, the Peoples Republic of China, Singapore, Yugoslavia, Bulgaria, Poland, the Soviet Union, Greece, Italy, Portugal, East Germany, West Germany, Norway, Sweden, Finland, Canada, and Argentina have all been known to build ships for export on credit terms. However, there is little that is unique about these programs: they generally are a variation on one of the types already described. A prospective buyer's best source of information is apt to be the shipyard at which it is planned to place the order.

Notes

1. Organization for Economic Cooperation and Development.

2. Throughout this book, the term ''security'' will be used in a broad sense to include personal or corporate guarantees, as well as liens on real assets.

3. A standby letter of credit is, literally, a letter addressed to a beneficiary by a bank. In this letter, the bank, as in a commercial letter of credit, promises to pay up to a specified amount to the beneficiary upon the beneficiary's presentation of certain documents specified in the letter. In ship financings, the specified documents typically include a draft, and a statement signed by an authorized officer of the beneficiary stating something to the effect that ''Borrower X is in default under the terms of a loan agreement dated XX/YY/ZZ.'' Thus, a standby letter of credit serves much the same purpose as a guarantee, but is conceptually rather different in that the bank is not required to make any determination that the borrower is actually in default. Its obligation is to verify that the documents presented are those required by the letter and, assuming they are in order, to make payment.

4. The term ''finance ratio'' will be used repeatedly in the book. Unless otherwise noted, it refers to the percentage of the contract price (in the case of a new building) or of the market value (in the case of a second hand vessel) financed.

5. Flag of convenience operations, while still very prevalent and economically attractive for a variety of reasons have come to suffer more and more from a particular disadvantage associated with crewing policies. Generally speaking, flag of convenience (f.o.c.) countries such as Liberia, Panama and Vanuatu do not regulate in any meaningful way the nationality of crews on vessels flying their flags. This results in opportunities for shipowners based in flag countries with high crewing costs to reduce operating costs by putting vessels under f.o.c.'s.

F.o.c. operations have, therefore, drawn the attention of the International Transport Workers Federation (I.T.F.), which has been seeking for years to establish a uniform wage standard for seamen working on f.o.c. vessels. To this end, the I.T.F. has brought increasingly successful actions against f.o.c. vessels calling in particular ports where the local labor environment is favorable. Though such actions can to a large extent be forestalled by obtaining an I.T.F. "blue card" (a documentary certification by the I.T.F. that the vessel complies with I.T.F. standards), there is increasing owner sentiment that the hassle is not worth it. Therefore, there is an increasing desire to put vessels under flags with a so-called "genuine link," i.e., the flag of operations is in some way genuinely linked to the vessel's ownership, management or normal trading zone in which case the I.T.F., as a matter of policy, will not interfere.

Given the fact that "genuine link" flags normally entail higher operating costs, it is easy to see that favorable financing programs can be a powerful incentive to choose one country over another. However, in most cases such programs are not sufficient. This is because of income taxation: f.o.c. vessels are not subject to income taxation, while most "genuine link" vessels are. Thus, programs such as the Belgian one have not been overwhelmingly successful. A Dutch program offering incentives based on operational subsidies rather than special financing has also not experienced overwhelming success. Two vessels placed under the Dutch flag by a U.S. based owner, for instance, were able to justify the move only because the owner knew that the state of the market would not allow the ships to be profitable, and therefore, they would not be subject to income tax in any case.

Chapter Three

Finance for Second-Hand Purchases: The Domination of Commercial Banks

Apart from operational and financial success, international sales and purchases of ships take place for a variety of reasons. First, patterns of trade may change, making a particular vessel no longer suitable for its owner's requirements. For example, the oversupply of very large crude carriers (VLCC's) was attributable in large part to the United States' shifting from the Arabian Gulf to Mexico as its major source of crude oil transported by sea. Mexican ports cannot accommodate VLCC's, and in any case, VLCC's are only economic for long voyages.

Second, there are certain maritime traditions of ownership that have an impact on ship sales. For instance, while Norwegian shipowners tend to acquire vessels by new construction, Greek shipowners tend to rely on second-hand purchases of older vessels (i.e. those viewed by their original builders as obsolescent). With the notable exception of Brazil, vessels purchased by shipowners in developing countries fit a similar pattern.

Third, the implementation of the UNCTAD[1] liner[2] code, which requires a 40%/40%/20%[3] allocation of cargo carriage among the importing country, exporting country, and third parties, has resulted in the transfer of some liner tonnage from traditional shipping countries to non-traditional countries. The Republic of Korea is a good example of a country that has gained tonnage in this way.

Similar proposals for cargo sharing in the bulk shipping area, if ever implemented, will have a parallel impact on bulkcarrier and tanker tonnage.

Lastly, with the depression in the shipping markets through most of the last decade, shipowners based in several of the countries with relatively high operating costs (such as most of the North European countries) have found that it is no longer economic to continue operations under their national flag. The result has been the transfer of a portion of their tonnage to flags with lower operating costs. The main beneficiaries of this have been Hong Kong Chinese owners operating under flags of convenience, which have inherited significant portions of the Norwegian and British fleets.

Though newbuilding finance is heavily dominated by official export credit agencies, it is clear that commercial banks also play a major direct or indirect role. In contrast, the role of export credit agencies in the financing of second-hand vessel purchases is minimal. The ECGD and the Spanish export agency have done a few, but the volume/value of such transactions is not significant.

With the exception of liner shipping (and often even in that sector), the typical shipowning group is composed of a series of companies. Usually, each ship is owned by a separate company. This is for reasons of limitation of liability: that is, when there is a multi-ship fleet, in theory action cannot be taken against one ship for debts or other legal responsibilities of another ship in the fleet. Most of the companies in the group exist solely to own a ship, and have little or no other financial substance except for a small amount of cash. The remaining companies in the group are apt to exist to carry out specific functions for all the vessels: brokerage, general management, crewing, agency, and insurance, for instance.

To make things more complicated, the single purpose nature of a shipowning company means that by definition, with the possible exception of a refinancing, the borrowing company has no financial track record as far as a lender is concerned. Furthermore, single purpose shipowning companies formed in most jurisdictions issue only bearer shares, and therefore their legal ownership cannot be proven.

The connecting link in such typical shipowning groups, is either a holding company, or common (or at least similar) share ownership of all the companies. In the first case, the relationship among the companies is well defined, and it may be possible to give substance to a financing by incorporating a holding company guarantee.

In the latter case, while the shareholdings should be known to the lender, they may not be provable. Furthermore, if the ownership of the companies in the group is in the hands of a family (as is often the case), the share ownership may well be spread among a large number of people, many of whom are likely to be inactive participants. By the same token, the percentages of ownership may not be the same for all companies in the group. The usual way to lend financial substance to a group of this sort is to incorporate the personal guarantees of one or more of the major shareholders (in the case of a family, one of these is likely, on the basis of counter-indemnities from other family members, to personally guarantee on behalf of the entire family). While professional lenders will endlessly debate the value of personal guarantees, it can at least be said that at most they are worth as much as the moral character of the people issuing them, and that at least they are useful as an embarrassment factor.

Because of the foregoing considerations, the typical form of commercial bank finance for vessel purchases is project finance (i.e. employment of the vessel is expected to be adequate to cover operating expenses and repay the debt), but with recourse to the corporate or individual parent. Recourse is required not only because the borrower is normally a single purpose company with little substance other than the vessel, but also because of risks with respect to employment. Security therefore takes the form of a mortgage over the vessel; assignments of the vessel's earnings and insurances; and the corporate guarantee of the parent company (if there is one), or, as it is frequently the case that the vessels in a shipowner's fleet are each owned by a separate company directly owned by the principal(s), the personal guarantee(s) of the shareholder(s).

Most commercial bank ship financings are on a variable rate Eurodollar basis, at a spread over the lender's LIBOR[4]. The interest rate is adjusted at the end of previously agreed upon periods, usually quarterly or semi-annually, but sometimes monthly or annually. Sometimes a lender will give a borrower the option to choose the relevant period, known as an interest period, at the end of which interest is payable. As the LIBOR's may vary depending on the interest period selected, the option scheme allows the borrower to attempt to minimize its interest cost according to its view as to the direction in which interest rates are moving.

Fixed rate commercial bank ship financings are difficult to come by. This is because commercial banks' primary sources of funds are on a variable rate basis. By agreeing to an interest rate fixed for the full life of the loan, the bank assumes a risk that interest rates will rise, thus putting it in a loss position. While in today's very sophisticated financial markets a bank ought to be able to execute an interest rate swap[5] to cover this risk, such a swap would normally be done only for the full term of the loan. If the loan is prepaid as the result of either the sale of the vessel or a refinancing, the lender may incur a loss from the necessity to enter into an offsetting swap for the remaining term of the loan. Therefore, a borrower wishing a commercial bank lender to quote a fixed rate should be prepared for the lender to require the borrower to indemnify it against such losses. It should also be aware that the swap will bear a cost, which is likely to result in a higher interest cost than might be available on a variable rate basis.

One option for a borrower concerned about its exposure to an upward movement in interest rates is to purchase a "cap." A cap is simply an agreement by a bank or other institution to pay all interest costs exceeding an agreed level. The cap is of course, available only at a price. The total cost of a cap, however, may be greatly reduced by purchasing both a cap and a "collar." A collar is simply an agreement by the borrower to pay to the bank (or other counterparty) the difference between an agreed floor level of interest and the actual level of interest, if the actual level is lower than the agreed floor. By purchasing both the cap and the collar, the cost of limiting (though not eliminating) exposure to interest rate movements, may be reduced by as much as two thirds.

Shipowners are occasionally dazzled by the possibility of reducing borrowing costs by borrowing in a currency other than U.S. dollars, or by borrowing U.S. dollars, but incorporating a multicurrency clause that allows the flexibility to periodically shift the currency of borrowing in an effort to take advantage of movements in exchange rates.

A borrowing in a currency other than U.S. dollars is for practical purposes the same in structure as a Eurodollar loan. Generally speaking it makes sense only in the exceptional circumstance in which a significant portion of the vessel's revenues is denominated in that currency.[6] Occasionally a time charter is denominated in a non-dollar currency, and certainly non-U.S. liner companies may have revenues in non-U.S. currencies.[7]

The multicurrency clause concept is rather more complicated. Typically, it uses a U.S. dollar borrowing amount as a collar, but gives the borrower the option to draw the loan for limited periods in other specified currencies. At the end of each period, the drawing must be repaid in full, plus an additional amount (if necessary) sufficient to reduce the total amount outstanding to no more than would have been outstanding had the loan been drawn in dollars. In contrast, however, if full repayment of the foreign currency drawing reduces the total amount outstanding to less than would have been outstanding had the drawing been in U.S. dollars, the difference is not usually available for re-drawing. By use of this collar concept, the lender is able to forestall unfavorable changes in the finance ratio that are attributable solely ɔ exchange rate movements. Some variation of a multicurrency clause may ıake economic sense if the vessel's revenues will be in a non-dollar currency or a period shorter than the full loan term, with the revenue currency of ucceeding periods unknown. Otherwise, apart from certain legal difficulties ı enforcing rights under mortgages securing loans with multi-currency lauses,[8] multicurrency clauses are nothing but a means to speculate in oreign currencies. Very few shipowners are equipped to do this to the same egree that they are equipped to speculate on ocean freight rates. Even rofessional foreign exchange traders incur their share of losses as well as ains. Furthermore, for every shipowner that has managed to benefit from multicurrency clause, there is at least one (and probably more) that has een hurt. Therefore, in most cases, such clauses are ill-advised.

Iost commercial bank ship financings provide for amortization of principal ı monthly, quarterly, or semi-annual installments. Some provide for grace eriods (i.e. periods without scheduled principal amortization) usually in the arly stages of a loan. This may be justified, for instance, when a financially rong shipowner wishes to take advantage of low ship purchase prices in weak freight market. The grace period allows it to acquire the vessel at favorable price, while avoiding the drain on the cash position of the emainder of the fleet that would result if the freight market were not ıfficiently strong to cover principal payments. However, a lender must be ıreful to ensure that the shipowner is really financially strong, and that there a mechanism for exerting pressure on the owner to access liquidity elsewhere the fleet if necessary. Such a mechanism could be the shipowner's corporate r personal guarantee; security interests in other vessels; and/or security in ther (non-shipping) assets.

ɔme commercial bank ship financings provide for "balloon" (lump sum) ayments at the final maturity of the loan. These may be justified in a full ayout loan if it is expected that the vessel will be scrapped at the final aturity. In this case, the lender must be careful that the amount of the alloon does not exceed the estimated scrap value of the vessel, conservatively lculated. Balloons may also be justified if the vessel's employment is ıknown beyond a certain stage, and the lender intends to refinance the alloon once the subsequent employment is known. In this case, the lender ust be very confident at the outset that when it comes time to refinance e balloon, the shipowner will still be a profitable (to the lender) and solvent ient. Since there may be a considerable time lapse between the initial loan ıd the refinancing, such a judgment may be rather problematical, and many nders (understandably) consequently feel very uncomfortable with this sort structure.

etween grace periods and balloons, there is a bewildering variety of possible incipal amortization schedules. For example, many shipowners are attracted by the apparent advantages of level payment loans: i.e. loans in which all payments, consisting of both interest and principal are equal. These are also known as annuity basis loans, and are similar in concept to home mortgages in the U.S. They can, of course, be done only on a fixed rate basis. Though the payments are level throughout the life of the loan, the allocation of the payments to interest and principal changes with each payment. The allocation is made according to a mathematical formula[9] known as the sum of the year's digits method. The practical effect is that in the early stages of the loan, the payments consist primarily of interest, and a relatively small amount of principal. Over time, the amount allocated to interest declines, and the amount allocated to principal increases, so that at the final maturity the payment consists largely of principal.

The obvious appeal of level payment loans is that their cash flow impact is both predictable and even. In jurisdictions subject to income tax, there is an additional appeal; with interest falling most heavily in the earlier stages of the loan, the tax deductibility of interest results in a favorable cash flow impact in the earlier stages when it is supposedly most needed.

The most common amortization schedule in commercial bank ship finance is level payments of principal, with interest (whether fixed or variable rate) additional. However, shipowners often advance the argument briefly noted above (that some cash flow relief is appropriate in the early stages of a loan) to support a request for uneven principal payments: lower in the early stages, and higher in the later stages. Banks seldom question this argument.

In fact, it is in both the lender's and shipowner's interest to tailor the debt service schedule as much as possible to the anticipated cash flow from operation of the vessel.[10] If the vessel is subject to a time charter with progressively escalating rates, then it may indeed be appropriate to structure a loan with lower principal payments in the earlier stages. In most cases however, such a structure has a hidden trap. Assuming that interest rates do not exceed the projected level in a variable rate transaction (and this can be ensured by purchase of a cap), the totals of principal and interest due will gradually decline because interest is payable on a declining oustanding principal payment. In contrast, vessel operating costs typically inflate to some degree from year to year. There is a trade-off here, and the ultimate outcome depends on the actual level of interest rates, and the actual inflation of operating costs. It is certainly not unusual for operating costs to escalate faster than total debt service declines. Therein lies the hidden trap, as it could very easily happen that with smaller principal payments in the earlier stages, total debt service would become heaviest at the same time that operating costs were peaking.

When a shipowner requests smaller principal payments in the earlier stages, the hidden intention is often (though not always) to allow some excess cash to be built up to cover working capital requirements. In fact, it should be the shipowner's responsibility to provide adequate working capital at the outset, and a lender should properly be suspicious if the shipowner is reluctant or unable to do so. In fact, a strong case can be made for structuring a loan with larger principal payments in the earlier stages, when operating costs are lower.

For those that believe in balance sheet analysis in conjunction with their assessment of ship financing transactions (and this is certainly valid for liner companies and some bulk companies) there is an accounting issue involved in the discussion of principal amortization. Simply stated, with any amortization schedule involving increasing payments of principal, the amount of debt shown on the balance sheet, and the reported future maturities of long term debt will be larger than they would be otherwise. This can have an unfavorable impact on leverage and coverage ratios.

The balance sheet issue is apt to be relevant primarily to public companies, and to liner companies, whether public or private. Despite everything noted above, the ultimate outcome of the principal/amortization debate depends on the relative negotiating strengths of borrower and lender.

The tenor or term of ship financings depends largely on the age of the vessel. In keeping with the project financing nature of these loans, it is important to the lender that the vessel have some useful life at the final maturity of the loan, and that the vessel be modern enough so that if a depressed market puts the owner in default, there is time for the vessel to regain value in the next upward market swing. Each lender has its own method of dealing with the age question, but a common rule of thumb is that a dry bulkcarrier has a useful life of twenty years, but that a tanker, because of its more technology intensive nature, has a useful life of only fifteen years. In other words, a fifteen year old bulkcarrier might be financed over five years, but a five-year old tanker might be financed over ten years. Most lenders view ten years as the maximum tenor, regardless of the age of the vessel, though a few may accept twelve years for a newbuilding.

The normal finance ratio in second-hand ship financing is 50-80% of the market value, depending on the form of vessel employment. Different forms of vessel employment pose differing degrees of risk with respect to the adequacy of the income for debt service. Reducing the percentage of finance compensates, at least in part, for increased employment risk.[11]

A few shipowners have been successful in inducing lenders to finance vess purchases on a non-recourse basis: i.e. without parent company o shareholder guarantees. Marine Transport Lines has pursued this approac particularly aggressively by assigning medium term time or bareboat charter In other cases, particularly with upper tier Greek shipowners, lenders hav been willing to forego personal guarantees in return for unusually low financ ratios (50-60%). Lastly, a few non-recourse transactions have been done o the basis of insuring the value of the vessel at the expiry of a charter th only partially covers repayment of the loans. Most financings, howeve continue to be done on a recourse basis.

Notes

1. United Nations Conference on Trade and Development.

2. Appendix A is a brief summary of types of vessel and their respective modes operation and employment. It is intended for those with no shipping indust background and all others should disregard it.

3. By bi-lateral agreement, some countries have agreed to splits differing from thi usually increasing the percentages for the importing and exporting countries at t expense of third parties.

4. London Interbank Offered Rate. This concept is subject to considerable confusi even among bankers. It does not represent the bank's cost of funds. The cost of fun is the LIBID rate, or the rate at which the bank is willing to bid for deposits fro clients or other banks. LIBOR is the rate at which the bank is willing to place deposi LIBOR is typically at a slight premium (1/16% to 1/8%) over the LIBID rate. Ban typically set their LIBOR's once daily. Most loan agreements call for the applicab rate to be the one quoted by the bank's London office at 11:00 a.m. two busine days prior to the beginning of an interest period.

5. An interest rate swap is simply an agreement between two parties to exchan streams of interest payments. The parties typically have offsetting requirements: o has an excess of variable rate funds and the other has an excess of fixed rate fund By agreeing to exchange the stream of interest payments on an agreed notion principal amount, each is able to move toward restoring a balance.

6. This argument deliberately ignores the possibility of simultaneously entering in offsetting foreign exchange futures contracts, or a foreign currency swap. Forei exchange futures contracts are simply agreements to purchase specified amounts the currency in question at specified dates in the future at preagreed exchange rat A currency swap, while serving much the same purpose, is conceptually somewh different. It is more comparable to an interest rate swap, but instead of swappi nterest payment flows, the parties swap currency payment flows. In either case, ship financings, because of their amortization schedules, tend to be difficult and hence expensive to find counterparties for. Thus, the cost of entering into the futures contracts or a swap tends to consume the potential for savings from lower interest rates.

From a theoretical perspective, it is worth noting that to a large degree movements in exchange rates are directly attributable to changes in the interest rate differential between the two relevant countries. Thus, even on a theoretical basis, the possibilities for achieving savings by borrowing in a non-dollar currency and hedging by way of futures or a swap are rather limited.

'. Both the shipowner and the ship financier must be careful to distinguish between the currency of exposure and the currency of collection. Most freight rates in the liner trades are set by reference to tariffs set by multinational conferences of shipowners. Because of the multinational nature of the membership, the tariffs must be set by reference to some common currency, usually the U.S. dollar. Thus, a line, even though it bills and collects freights in local currencies, may well be protected from exchange rate exposure by the implicit indexation of its freight rates to the U.S. dollar.

. This difficulty arises because of requirements to specify the sum secured (the "sum certain" in legal jargon). With a multicurrency clause, the sum secured cannot be precisely specified without registering amendments to the mortgage each time the loan is repaid and drawn in a new currency. At best this procedure is very cumbersome, and at worst, lower ranking mortgages may have been registered in the meantime, thus jeopardizing the priority of the first mortgage. Even if the body of law governing the mortgage provides specifically for multicurrency clauses, the same issue may arise if, as is apt to be the case, the lender attempts to enforce the mortgage outside the flag country. This is because Article 1(c) of the Brussels Convention of 1967 provides in relevant part as follows:

> " 'Mortgages' and 'hypotheques' on sea-going vessels shall be enforceable in contracting states provided that:
>
> (c) either the register or any instruments referred to... above specifies... the amount secured..."

Numerous legal opinions have interpreted this to mean that the mortgage must secure a sum certain, and therefore, it could be argued, in an enforcement action outside the flag state but in a state that is a party to the Brussels Convention, that the mortgage is invalid.

9. Following are the various formulas pertaining to annuity basis loans:

a. Principal: $PV = PMT . \frac{1-(1+i)^{-n}}{i}$

b. Payment: $PMT = PV . \frac{i}{1-(1+i)^{-n}}$

c. Number of Periods: $n = \frac{\log\left(1 - i . \frac{PV}{PMT}\right)}{\log(1+i)}$

d. Interest Rate: Approximation formulas by Newton's Law.

With respect to the above PV = amount borrowed; PMT = payment amount; i = interest rate; and n = number of payment periods. The allocation of payments to interest and principal can be determined from the following formulas:

e. $INT_n = BAL_{n-1} . i$

f. $PRN_n = PMT - INT_n$

g. $BAL_n = BAL_{n-1} - PRN_n$

Where INT_n = interest payable in period n; BAL_n = remaining principal balance at the end of period n; i = interest rate; and PRN_n = principal payable in period n. To preserve some semblance of sanity, it is prudent to leave these calculations to a business calculator or appropriate computer software.

10. Chapter VII includes a lengthy discussion of how to project cash flows.

11. See Appendix A.

Chapter Four

The United States: A Special Case

The U.S. flag merchant fleet is one of the most heavily subsidized (and hence politicized) fleets in the world but nevertheless its economic performance has generally been dismal. The principal ingredients in this poor performance have been very high crewing costs; the world's highest vessel construction costs (until relatively recently, the only vessels eligible for registry under the U.S. flag were those constructed in the U.S.); and in some respects technological obsolescence.

The political response to these problems has been in the form of various subsidy programs. These include Operating Differential Subsidies (ODS), under which shipowners using U.S. crews in international trading enter into contracts with a U.S. government agency to compensate at least in theory for the difference between the cost of U.S. crew and the cost of other nationalities of crew. In return, the shipowner agrees to maintain certain specified levels of service on specified trade routes. In recent years, the Reagan administration has attempted, with only limited success, to phase this program out. There have even been situations in which shipowners reached tentative agreement with the U.S. government agency involved to buy out their ODS contracts at a discount, thus putting an end to the government's funding requirement, and relieving the owner of the service requirements, which had to be met whether or not they were profitable. In fact, however, most of these tentative agreements failed in the end.

To address the high construction cost issue, the Construction Differential Subsidy (CDS) program was implemented to, again, at least in theory, compensate for the difference between construction costs in the U.S. and construction costs elsewhere. In this respect, it is worth noting that a vessel constructed in the U.S. will often cost up to three times the cost of a similar vessel constructed in Japan or Korea. Thus, the differential is not an issue of insignificant magnitude. The CDS never satisfactorily addressed this differential, and accordingly, the U.S. merchant fleet quickly became overaged. Added to this was the Reagan administration's desire to phase out the program, as a result of which it was underfunded. On the other hand, the Reagan administration opened the door for U.S. shipowners to order abroad. This was a very important development, and will be referred to again further on.

The U.S. flag commercial fleet became overaged as the result of owner's inability to replace vessels at a competitive cost. The vessels themselves therefore became uncompetitive on a technological basis. Though research and development subsidies were made available, their impact was minimal. Even today, most U.S. flag vessels continue to be powered by turbine engines, whereas the rest of the world relies mainly on much more fuel efficient diesel engines.

Other direct and indirect subsidies[1] to the U.S. flag fleet include flag preference, and lucrative charters. Flag preference refers to restriction of cargo movements between or among U.S. ports to unsubsidized U.S. flag vessels under the Jones Act.[2] It also refers to bi-lateral cargo sharing agreements with other countries, reserving a share of the cargo movements between the U.S. and the relevant country to U.S. flag vessels.[3] It further refers to the restriction of all or a portion of certain "government impelled" cargoes, such as military materiel movements and subsidized export programs for developing countries under PL480, to U.S. flag vessels. In addition, the U.S. Navy maintains a fleet of merchant vessels intended to operate in support of international military movements. Under the auspices of the Military Sealift Command (MSC), a significant portion of this fleet has traditionally been owned and operated by the private sector under time charters to the MSC. Because these vessels must fly the U.S. flag, and consequently incur U.S. costs; because the MSC typically insists upon rather special vessel specifications requiring additional investments in the vessel; and because the MSC, as a matter of policy, wants vessel operations to be profitable enough to ensure its required level of service, these charters tend to be at very profitable rates.

In addition to the foregoing, U.S. flag vessels are theoretically entitled to financing (for new construction) under Title XI. Title XI provides for the most generous financing terms in the world: 80% of the construction cost (after CDS), repayable over twenty-five years. The shipowner issues bonds in this amount and term under a U.S. government guarantee (it is thus the government that holds the mortgage). The benefits do not end there: typically these transactions are done without recourse, so that many a U.S. flag shipowner, when finding that a vessel is no longer economic, has simply turned the vessel over to the government without being held responsible for the remaining debt.

The Title XI program, like the other subsidy programs, is in the process of being phased out. In fact, today the program is not only largely unfunded, but is heavily in debt to the U.S. Treasury, from which it has been forced to borrow in order to repay in excess of $1 billion of Title XI bonds that would otherwise be in default.

In summary, aside from military contracts, there is presently very little tonnage under construction in the United States; the only commercially viable business is viable only because of subsidy; the fleet, though its age profile has improved, is still overaged; what fleet renewal there has been in recent years has been largely constructed abroad without subsidy; and the number of commercially viable operators has contracted as the result of consolidation, or in some cases, financial failure. It is clear that the subsidy programs have not worked, and in fact the only serious grounds that are advanced for continuing them are based on national security: the perceived need to maintain a U.S. flag fleet (and shipbuilding capacity) in the event of war. Even in this respect there is considerable debate, as a strong case can be made that U.S. controlled flag of convenience tonnage would be available in time of war. Even the MSC has in recent years begun to charter foreign built tonnage (though flying the U.S. flag).

This is the background to the U.S. ship financing scene. How does one finance an industry that has been performing so poorly?

As noted above, most of the fleet renewal in recent years has been accomplished by way of foreign construction. In addition to reducing vessel construction costs, this has thrown the U.S. flag operators into the world of conventional ship finance, from which they were formerly insulated by the Title XI program. The adjustment has not been easy. The U.S. Lines case is instructive in this respect.

In the early 1980's as part of its efforts to introduce an "around the world service" (ATWS), U.S. Lines (U.S.L.) placed an order in Korea for twelve new container ships. At the time, these were the largest container ships ever ordered or built. It was successful in arranging 100% finance for this order: 50% was provided by the Export Import Bank of Korea, under standby letters of credit issued by a syndicate of U.S. commercial banks, which in turn held first mortgages over the vessels; 30% was provided by the shipyard, which held second mortgages; and the balance was provided by a major U.S.

commercial finance company and a major U.S. insurance company, which held third and fourth mortgages as security. After placing this order, U.S.L proceeded to make two acquisitions. It first bought Moore McCormack Lines again with 100% financing: a combination of redeemable preferred stock held by Moore McCormack's former parent, Moore McCormack Resources, and a loan from another U.S. money center commercial bank. Then it proceeded to acquire the routes and newbuilding contracts previously owned by Delta Steamship. The financing for this transaction is less clear, but all of the newbuilding contracts which represented the bulk of the purchase price, were subject to official export credits.

U.S.L. started the decade as an abnormally leveraged concern. This was the result of the fact that when McLean Industries acquired it from Walter Kidde in the late 1970's, much of the acquisition financing was in the form of debt provided by a major U.S. insurance company. The fleet renewal and additional acquisition financings were on top of this, so that as the ATWS came on stream in the mid-1980's, the company was very highly leveraged.

Unfortunately for U.S.L., it was not the only operator in the world that was enamored of the ATWS concept. Another pioneer of the concept was Evergreen Marine, based in Taipei, Republic of China. Evergreen's concept was slightly different: it operated a larger number of relatively small (but still large in absolute terms) ships, and sent them around the world in both directions rather than just one, in order to provide a more frequent service. In addition, as its vessels were flying (primarily) the Panamanian flag rather than the U.S. flag, Evergreen had a much lower operating cost profile.

The world market was not yet large enough to accommodate two such new services on such a large scale. As might be expected, a freight rate price war ensued, as both operators struggled to keep their vessels full. However, U.S.L. had to work harder: both companies were leveraged, but Evergreen had both more favorable costs and a frequency of service advantage.

At the time of writing Evergreen is apparently profitable, while U.S.L. has declared bankruptcy. It is thus clear that even with modern tonnage, when operating outside of protected trades, the U.S. flag fleet continues to be plagued by its traditional bogeymen of high operating costs and under-capitalization.

The other major U.S. flag liner operators all perceive a need for major fleet renewal programs. Lykes Lines is perhaps the most desperate, and apart from partial contraction of its operations, its plans are not clear. American President Lines (APL) announced a $500 million vessel renewal program over the next few years: the financing arrangements are not yet clear, but fortunately APL has a relatively strong balance sheet. Sea Land also has a need for fleet renewal, and has bought the large U.S. Lines vessels. It plans to reduce their capacity, and enter into charters with other lines in order to ensure usage of excess capacity.

Among the liner companies, APL is probably in the strongest position. However, it is a subsidized operator, and if the ODS program is ever closed out, its future will become rather more doubtful. The others, with the exception of Lykes which is privately owned, are, like APL, independent public companies which are nevertheless finding it extremely difficult to find the necessary capital. One solution may be to seek to be acquired by larger, stronger public companies, preferably ones involving some element of synergy. Sea Land, which has been acquired by the CSX Corporation, seems to be going this route, but there is some thought that the acquirer may not fully appreciate the scale of the required new capital investment. In any case, the history of ownership of U.S. liner companies by non-shipping concerns has been less than happy: APL by Natomas Corporation; Lykes Line by LTV Corporation; Sea Land by R.J. Reynolds; Delta Steamship by Holiday Inns; U.S. Lines by Walter Kidde; and various others that could be named. In each case, it appears that the non-shipping parent underestimated the capital requirements.

The outlook for U.S. flag liner shipping is rather grim, though official export credits will continue to play a role for the foreseeable future. The real problem is on the equity side, although the development of a considerably longer term debt instrument would be helpful. One reason for the lack of this is the investment banking community's lack of interest in the shipping sector (see Chapter VI).

Outside of transactions involving long term firm employment, and/or operation in protected trades, the outlook for U.S. flag bulk shipping is even grimmer. A significant portion of the dry bulk fleet in the Great Lakes (Jones Act) is laid up, a fact which speaks for itself. The coastwise Jones Act dry bulk fleet is so small that it cannot be seriously discussed. What little international dry bulk tonnage there is, is either grossly overaged, or economically uncompetitive.

The U.S. flag tanker fleet presents a somewhat different picture. In the late 1970's and very early 1980's, a good deal of unsubsidized tanker tonnage was built primarily to move Alaskan oil to the lower forty-eight states, a movement subject to the Jones Act. Most of this tonnage was built by major oil companies, or by independent operators with long term time charters to major oil companies. The financing was mostly done under Title XI, or by way of leveraged leases (see Chapter V) in which the debt factor was Title XI bonds.

To the extent that the aforementioned charters have not expired these vessels continue to be viable business. However, to the extent that they are coming open, they are vulnerable. This is a good example of the difficulties involved in depending on a protected market.

The heart of the present problem is that in the late 1970's a number of subsidized U.S. flag tankers were also constructed. They were, of course, intended for international trading, based on the Carter administration's plans to build up a Strategic Petroleum Reserve, and on expectations that Alaskan oil would be exported to Japan. The Strategic Petroleum Reserve program was allowed to lapse much sooner than anticipated, and the Alaskan oil exports never materialized. Those subsidized tankers without long term employment came open immediately, and those with long term employment are coming open now. In both cases, their owners are eyeing the profitable Jones Act business from Alaska, which is still undertonnaged, and hence profitable. Though permitted to operate in the Alaskan trade on a temporary basis from time to time, but then only when there is insufficient unsubsidized tonnage available, the subsidized tankers have been leading a precarious existence. Many of their owners have applied to repay the subsidies, in order to qualify to trade full time on a Jones Act basis. The existing unsubsidized operators are, of course, taking action to have these applications denied, as they foresee a resulting weakening of the market.

Once again, the ultimate outcome is unclear. For the future, with an unreliable market, no subsidies available, and virtually no Title XI money available, it is difficult to see any reason why new orders would be placed, except perhaps occasionally by an oil company for its own captive requirements, or perhaps for charter to the MSC. In the absence of a protected trade, U.S. flag tankers have not been competitive in the international market for years. Financing is not really a significant factor.

All of the discussion so far in this chapter has been related directly or indirectly to financing for new construction. There is very little in the way of a second hand market in U.S. flag vessels. This is largely because of the historical prevalence of Title XI financing, and related requirements that vessels be kept for rather lengthy minimum periods of time. A tendency developed for these vessels to be upgraded or otherwise modified, rather than sold for further trading.

What little second hand selling and purchasing has been done has usually be financed by commercial banks in the manner described in Chapter III. The principal difference has been that lenders have been forced to take a more liberal view on vessel age, as most of these vessels have been much older than those normally bought and sold in the international market. This set of circumstances is apt to change as U.S. flag shipowners are allowed more and more access to the worldwide sale and purchase market.

High vessel construction costs in the U.S. have made U.S. vessels totally uncompetitive in the export market. Only a few high technology vessels (mostly LNG carriers) have been exported. Generally speaking, the U.S. Export-Import Bank has been reluctant to finance these exports.

Notes

1. For one reason or another, the world's shipowners typically have an effective income tax rate of zero. In the U.S., this is achieved primarily by means of the Capital Construction Fund (CCF). Basically, a U.S. flag shipowner is permitted to indefinitely postpone taxation on income provided that the funds are set aside in a CCF for the purpose of servicing debt, constructing new U.S. flag tonnage, or upgrading existing tonnage. The CCF concept is not emphasized here, because most non-U.S. flag shipowners also benefit from some device that makes them effectively, if not theoretically tax exempt. Likewise, CCF's cannot be used for foreign construction, and hence, are likely to become increasingly irrelevant.

2. To be fair, it must be noted that this kind of cabotage law is the rule rather than the exception in countries having any significant degree of coastline.

3. Direct subsidies are available only for vessels trading in international competition. Thus, vessels engaged in Jones Act trading, or which are involved in government impelled cargoes (including Strategic Petroleum Reserve movements) are not eligible for subsidies.

Chapter Five

Leasing: Inexpensive Finance or Source of Equity

For the purposes of this discussion, the essential nature of a lease is that it is a financing transaction. This distinguishes it from an operating lease, which is more akin to a voyage or time charter. Under a finance lease, the lessee is responsible for all physical operations and insurance, leaving the lessor responsible only for finance.

There are two reasons for a shipowner to engage in a leasing transaction. First, most shipowners are subject to an effective income tax rate of zero percent. For flag of convenience owners, this is literally true. In other (taxable) jurisdictions it happens for a variety of reasons, such as favorable depreciation rates, investment tax credits, capital construction funds, or other similar devices. As the owner's fleet expands, there may be insufficient taxable income to fully use the deductions associated with ownership. By leasing the vessel instead, the owner may be able to transfer these deductions to an investor that can use them, receiving in return a corresponding benefit in the effective finance cost. All this is achieved without giving up control of the vessel. The second reason for engaging in a lease is to raise the equity portion of a financing.

Most ship leases are so called leveraged leases, in which an investor(s) puts up 20%-40% of the total purchase price (the equity portion). Typically a bank acts as a trustee on the investors' behalf.

The balance of the purchase price is raised in some form of debt. This debt, which is without recourse to the investor(s), is secured by a mortgage on the ship, and an assignment of the lease payments. The lease payments are structured so as to exactly cover the debt service requirements, plus provide a return to the investor(s) in either cash or tax benefits. The latter almost always include depreciation, investment tax credits (if applicable) and interest, but a portion of the investor(s) return may also be the residual value of the vessel at the expiry of the lease. Leases may be structured with or without renewal options, and with or without purchase options. Purchase options may be at a pre-agreed price, or at "fair market value" at the time of purchase.

The precise calculations of lease payments vary from jurisdiction to jurisdiction depending on the specifics of the applicable tax law, the specific structure and timing of the transaction, and the interest rate on the debt. They are also rather complicated, and sometimes can only be effectively done with a computer model.[1]

Tax based leasing of ships used to be done quite actively in the United States, using the leverage provided by Title XI bonds. Transactions may have been done based on leverage from official export programs, but there was considerable reluctance on the part of the agencies involved to transfer the credit from the party originally ordering the vessel to a relatively anonymous group of investors, even though the credit risk was for practical purposes the same. U.S. tax based leasing has been limited (with one possible exception described further on) to vessels flying the U.S. flag, although it is worth noting by liner operations that leasing is a favored means of acquiring containers.

The United Kingdom has also had an active leasing program, but once again, only for British flag vessels. There was, for a short time a few years ago, a structure that made it possible to take advantage of both U.S. and U.K. tax benefits, but the Inland Revenue quickly discovered the "loopholes" and closed them. Thus, today U.K. tax leveraged leases are attractive only in rather limited circumstances.

In a number of other countries, particularly in Norway and Germany, the limited partnership is a very accepted means of raising capital for investment in tonnage flying the same flag. Often the investment is leveraged. If the vessel is then chartered on an extended period basis (not always the case), these transactions may take on some of the character of tax leveraged leases. However, in these transactions the capital raising purpose usually takes precedence over the tax benefit purpose.

As is apparent from the foregoing examples, cross border tax leases (i.e. leases arranged with capital being provided by one country for investmen in ships flying the flags of other countries) are very difficult to arrange. Thi is because the tax benefits are usually available only for "domestic' investments. However, there are a few possible exceptions.

First, the phraseology of one section of the U.S. tax law is somewha ambiguous with respect to equipment employed in the foreign trade of th U.S. Tax specialists have held that if the lessee of containers is a U.S. line company, that fact is prima facie evidence that the containers are employe in the foreign trade of the U.S. Some feel that the lessee must be a U.S company. Others, however, argue that if the containers touch U.S. shore a certain minimum number of times per year, the nationality of the lesse is irrelevant. It is on the basis of this argument that a major U.S. mone center bank arranged a container leveraged lease for Evergreen Marine Though the foregoing pertains to containers, one can perceive a basis fo making the same argument with respect to vessels. It must be emphasize that the tax basis for the above is subject to considerable disagreement. Th second example is also subject to considerable disagreement.

Over the last few years, several transactions, usually involving tankers, hav ben arranged with capital from the U.S. being invested in flag of convenienc tonnage. The vessels were purchased by Liberian corporations and flew th Liberian flag. The Liberian corporations bareboat chartered (i.e., lease without tax benefit or operating responsibility) the ships to one or more Ne York State limited partnerships. The bareboat charters contained purchas options at a price U.S. $1.00 in excess of whatever amount would be require to fully satisfy loans secured by mortgages taken out to finance a portio of the original acquisition (this structure was intended to provide a basis fo arguing that the beneficial ownership was U.S., and therefore the tax benefit of ownership could be legitimately passed to the partners). The limite partnerships then time chartered the vessels to third parties, giving th transactions much of the character of tax leveraged leases.

The partnership offerings were deliberately held to thirty-five units presumably so as to avoid the costs of review by the U.S. Securities an Exchange Commission (SEC). As a result, the tax structure has yet to b tested, and the untested issues are freely acknowledged in the prospectus If the tax structure stands up, this concept could become a major source o ship finance in the future. At least one major New York law firm, however feels that the structure will not stand up.

Apart from the above, little leasing is done in the international market, excep where the purpose is solely to arrange the equity. The lack of tax benefit for the owner, which is usually a company incorporated in Liberia or Panama, is therefore reflected in higher pricing. Transactions of this sort are usually referred to as bareboat charters, the charterer being responsible for all physical operations and insurance, and the owner responsible only for finance. The transactions are also usually on a "full payout" basis: that is, the charterer is committed for a period sufficient to fully pay for the vessel (assuming there is debt involved), though not necessarily for its full useful life. Likewise, the finance ratios tend to be high (sometimes even 100%) if the charterer is believed to be very strong financially. Bareboat charters used to be the core business of Papachristides Maritime, formerly based in Montreal, and now headquartered in London, though in recent years Papachristides has moved more and more into conventional spot, time charter, and ship management operations. Other bareboat charter business is done in bits and pieces by a variety of owners.

Though it does not necessarily involve leasing in any way, there is a tax based vehicle that may be useful for raising capital in the U.S. for investment in non U.S. flag tonnage. This vehicle is the "non-controlled foreign corporation."[2]

Under present U.S. income tax law, a U.S. taxpayer[3] must report and pay tax on his, her or its share of certain types of earnings of any non-U.S. corporation which is directly or indirectly controlled by U.S. taxpayers, regardless of whether or not he, she or it received any cash income from that corporation. However, if the non-U.S. corporation is not directly or indirectly controlled by U.S. taxpayers, the U.S. taxpaying shareholders are subject to tax only on earnings distributed in cash. Thus, by offering to U.S. taxpayers an investment in a non-controlled corporation, capital may be raised by making available an effective and legal tax deferral scheme.[4]

There are two ways for a non-U.S. corporation to qualify as non-controlled. First (and simplest), the transaction may be arranged such that 50% of its shares are owned by non-U.S. taxpayers. It is understood that the U.S. tax authorities will accept 50% non-U.S. taxpaying ownership as prima facie evidence that the corporation is not U.S. controlled. Second (and more interesting), if the sum of all U.S. taxpayers' shareholdings amounting individually to 10% or more of the shares outstanding is less than 50%, it is understood that the U.S. tax authorities will still take the view that the corporation is not U.S. controlled. Thus, it is legally feasible to establish a non-U.S. corporation owned entirely by U.S. taxpaying investors, while preserving non-U.S. controlled tax status.

By creating a shipowning company that qualifies as a non-controlled corporation, or by creating a shipowning company itself owned by a partnership that qualifies as non-controlled, it may be possible to incorporate an element of tax benefit that would otherwise be missing in international ship leasing transactions.

Notes

1. *The Handbook of Leasing: Techniques and Analysis* (Petrocelli Books, Inc., 1982), by Terry A. Isom and Sudhir P. Amembal is an excellent though now outdated exposition of the technical details of all kinds of leasing.

2. Though this discussion will be couched in terms of a corporation, it is understood that the rules applying to partnerships are substantially the same.

3. The ensuing discussion deliberately refers to U.S. taxpayers rather than U.S. citizens. Many non-U.S. citizens have income taxable in the U.S., and the ''non-controlled foreign corporation'' may be particularly attractive to such taxpayers.

4. It is not yet clear whether the Tax Reform Act of 1986 will have any impact on this concept.

Chapter Six

The Ship Financing Institutions and Intermediaries

Any discussion of institutions active in ship finance must be qualified to the extent that it is not yet possible to fully assess the damage the commercial banks have suffered as the result of the recent severe depressions in virtually all of the shipping markets. With one minor exception (noted below), involvement in ship finance has so far never been known to cause the failure of a commercial bank, though in at least one case it was definitely a contributing factor. The real damage has been in ship financing departments' credibility with their managements. Virtually all of the traditional ship financing banks are presently either inactive or selective in the extreme when considering new ship financing transactions, and the extent to which they will return to active involvement if and when markets improve is problematical. For now, most are forced to be content with "licking their wounds."

The commercial banks that have traditionally been active in ship finance, most of which have had specialist departments for this purpose, have tended to be large money center banks because of the large capital commitments that this business requires. Most of the large U.S. banks have been involved: Citibank, Chase Manhattan, Morgan Guaranty, Chemical, Bankers Trust, First National Chicago, Marine Midland, Irving Trust, Manufacturers Hanover, the Bank of America, and the Bank of Boston. They have been active not only in the U.S., but in all the other major shipping markets: Greek, Scandinavian, and Hong Kong Chinese. Much the same can be said with respect to the major U.K. banks, but Midland, Standard Chartered, National Westminster, Barclays, Hambros, National and Grindlays, and William and Glyns are the best known.

The U.S. and U.K. banks dominate the market but there are a number of banks based in other countries that have also been active, and not only in their own countries. For instance, Den norske Bank (formerly Den Norske Creditbank) has been active in the United States, though mostly with offshore drilling rigs and supply vessels, and Christiana Bank og Kreditkasse has also been active, though mostly with Norwegian shipowners. Banque de Paris et des Pays Bas used to be very active, particularly in the Far East, and Credit Commercial and Banque Indosuez made an entree to the market a few years ago. The Greek market has been heavily dominated by non-Greek banks, but the National Bank of Greece has done some ship financing. The Japanese banks have generally limited their ship financing activities to Japanese shipowners, but have engaged in some ship export financing on behalf of their shipyard clients.

Lastly, the Hong Kong and Shanghai has also been active, but primarily with Hong Kong Chinese shipowners.

In general, the list of active banks has varied little. Chemical maintained a low profile for a few years following a difficult workout in Norway, but subsequently returned in a surprisingly aggressive posture. Continental Illinois, whose traditional involvement was a significant contributing factor to its near failure, is no longer active in ship finance.

On a smaller scale, the Colonial Bank (a Connecticut regional bank) was very active for a while, but when ship loan problems forced it to successfully solicit a "bailout" from the Bank of Boston, it for practical purposes dropped out of the market. The Algemene Bank Nederland, though a large bank, developed only a modest portfolio outside Holland. Severe problems with its Greek portfolio caused it to cut back its activity to a trickle. In contrast, the Union Trust Company (another Connecticut regional bank) began doing some ship financing a few years ago, mostly with middle tier Greeks. As noted above, Credit Commercial and Indosuez entered the market, but their marketing thrusts never became clear.

In addition to the commercial banks, there have been a number of specialist ship finance companies. Generally, these companies have funded themselves with commercial paper, bank borrowings, or floating rate notes, and have tended to focus on the higher risk sector of the ship finance market. The best known of these are the German and Dutch ship mortgage "banks" (Sheepshypotheeken zu Lubeck and Nederlandse Scheepshypotheek Bank,[1] for instance), and the Oceanic Finance Corporation, which is Bermuda based with Canadian shareholders, but managed to a large degree from London.

A few of the U.S. commercial finance companies have also been active in ship finance. In most cases, their involvement began with U.S. flag leasing which they found very profitable. When they expanded into general ship finance, however, the required yields were based on a comparison with the high yields on leases. In order to achieve these yields, they, like the specialists, have tended to focus on the high risk, high leverage sector of the market. In addition to normal loan interest, they have often required an "equity kicker" as additional compensation. The best known of these finance companies is the General Electric Credit Corporation, but CIT Financial and Greyhound Leasing have also been involved.

In general, the investment banking community has served the shipping industry very badly. To a large degree, this appears to be because of memories of Tidal Marine, a famous workout case in which a number of investment banks incurred losses. In any case, apart from the very occasional share issue for the very small sector consisting of publicly traded shipowners, the investment banking community, particularly in the U.S., has done little of note for shipowners whether publicly or privately held.[2] Even the Overseas Shipholding Group, which has as fine a track record as any, has arranged all of its debt with commercial banks, the U.S. government (Title XI), and official export credit agencies. In London, investment banking interest in shipping is slightly better. Kleinwort Benson, which features an ex-P&O[3] director on its board, is perhaps the best known, but the names Henry Ansbacher and Samuel Montagu (see below) crop up from time to time.

Generally speaking, large shipowners with a track record of experience have a need for an intermediary only when they are in financial difficulties. This situation is likely to change only if and when the investment banking community develops a saleable debt instrument having a tenor more closely approximating the useful life of a vessel.[4] However, smaller shipowners with a limited financial staff, new entrants to the market, or owners who for other reasons (such as an operating base in a developing country) lack direct access to the international capital markets, may well be able to benefit from the assistance of a professional financial intermediary.[5] Such intermediaries usually work on the basis of a modest upfront fee, plus a commission representing a percentage of the amount of financing arranged. A few work strictly on a contingency basis, and some will accept an equity position in the project in lieu of all or a portion of their compensation. In return for this compensation, the intermediary prepares a presentation for the financial institutions and/or other investors, introduces the owner to the institutions and/or investors, and, assuming that the necessary financing is forthcoming, assists if required with documentation.

The qualification at the beginning of this chapter concerning banks active in ship finance applies to intermediaries as well. Nevertheless, there are a number, headed in the main by former commercial banking officers, that appear to still be active.

The intermediaries are heavily concentrated in New York and London. The New York based intermediaries include DAC Associates, Inc., Interlink Agencies, Ltd. (actually Bermuda based), and Day & Partners. DAC is headed by Mr. Don Conzo (ex-Irving Trust), and has specialized in arranging equity and bank finance for second-hand vessels purchased by small operators. Interlink is headed by Mr. Paul Gurtler (ex-Marine Midland), and also specializes in arranging bank finance for the purchase of second-hand vessels by small to medium sized operators. Day & Partners is a relative newcomer to the market. Headed by Ms. Randee Day Ammon (ex-Morgan Guaranty), its specialty is not yet established.

Operating with offices in both New York and London is First International Capital Corporation (FICC). As reported in the press, FICC is 70% owned by a company controlled by Mr. Paul Slater, and 30% directly or indirectly owned by Henry Ansbacher, Ltd. Slater (ex-National and Grindlays; ex-original Managing Director of the Oceanic Finance Corporation; ex-head of Henry Ansbacher's U.S. subsidiary) is the managing head of the joint venture. Slater has historically built his client base from among the users (as distinguished from the owners) of vessels, and it appears that FICC will fit the same pattern.

The exclusively London based intermediaries include Shipping Finance, Ltd., Finance for Shipping, Ltd., and OSI Investments, Ltd. Shipping Finance, Ltd. is a subsidiary of Samuel Montagu, and is headed by Mr. Malcolm Savage (ex-Oceanic Finance). It is closely associated with major ship and insurance brokers. Finance for Shipping, Ltd. is understood to be controlled by Banque Louis Dreyfus. It is headed by Mr. Edward Harris, and is active primarily in continental Europe. OSI Investments is headed by Mr. Emanuel Kyprios (ex-Marine Midland, ex-Finansco, Ltd.).

In addition to the foregoing, it should be noted that the Oceanic Finance from time to time also acts as an intermediary/consultant.

Notes

1. Now a wholly owned subsidiary of Rabobank Nederland N.V., Amsterdam.

2. The recent public offering of shares in Majestic Shipping Co., Ltd. was possible only because Majestic was sponsored by the much larger Loews Corporation, which was to own 66-2/3% of the Majestic shares. Morgan Stanley and Merrill Lynch Capital Markets were the lead underwriters.

3. The old and famous Peninsular and Oriental Steam Navigation Company.

4. In this connection, it is interesting to speculate as to whether given the recent interest of oil companies in issuing oil indexed bonds (bonds with amortization schedules related to the performance of an index of oil prices: i.e., with amortization requirements at their highest when oil prices are at their highest), the investment banking community can come up with a freight rate indexed bond. The necessary indexes already exist and such a concept would greatly assist shipowners in managing their rather cyclical cash flow.

5. As distinguished from shipbrokers, who in conjunction with their sale and purchase efforts, often offer introductions to financial institutions.

Chapter Seven

The Analysis of the Ship Financing Transaction

The analysis of a ship financing transaction varies greatly depending on the type of vessel involved. When an owner purchases a bulkcarrier or tanker, for instance, the purchasing company is typically newly formed and, therefore has no financial track record. Analysis must focus on the market prospects for that type of vessel and on the guarantees available, if any, rather than on financial statements. Even in a refinancing, when there is a financial track record, financial statement analysis is of very limited value: vessels are carried on the balance sheet at depreciated historical cost, rather than at market value; revenues are determined by charters entered into in the past, and in the absence of a continuing period charter, have little relevance when assessing ability to repay debt in the future; and profit is distorted by depreciation charges related to vessel acquisition costs. In fact, when analyzing bulk shipping refinancings, the principal value in analyzing the financial statements is the ability to compare historical and projected operating costs, and to determine (when employment is on a time charter basis) what the historical level of offhire has been, and so calculate one indicator of operating performance. They also have some value in monitoring performance after a loan has been made.

The one situation in which financial statement analysis could have significantly greater value is when assessing the performance of a shipowning group as a whole. To be useful, the statements involved should be prepared on a consolidated basis,[1] but such statements are only rarely available. They are available primarily from publicly traded companies, and occasionally from larger, relatively sophisticated privately held companies.

In contrast, the analysis of ship financings in the liner sector depends heavily, although far from exclusively, on financial statement analysis. Though liner companies' financial statements also suffer from drawbacks relating to the historical vessel acquisition costs and related depreciation charges, these difficulties can be overcome. By definition, however, the performance of a liner company is related to its success in marketing a transportation service involving multiple vessels over a period of time, not just to the performance of a single ship. In other words, one must assess the performance of the line, not just the ships, and this can only be done through analysis of the financial track record on a consolidated basis.

Consequently, this chapter will be broken into two main analytical sections corresponding to bulk shipping and liner shipping. These will be followed by relatively brief sections on vessel operating pools and country risk. For ease of reference, Appendix B is a suggested list of materials that should be included in presentations to lenders.

Before proceeding to these sections, though, it is worth taking note of two issues common to both sectors. The first is the issue of audited financial statements. There is no excuse for a lender not requiring or a borrower not providing financial statements audited by an accounting firm of internationally recognized favorable reputation. While there is a cost attached, the preparation of accounting figures according to internationally accepted standards should lend a great deal of comfort to the lender/borrower relationship.[2] Likewise, it puts the relationship on an impartial, professional basis, which is much to be desired, particularly as the shipowning operation grows to an extent that it requires the support of multiple lenders. If the related loss of confidentiality is important enough to a shipowner, it is probably better not to borrow at all. Even shipowners in developing countries can usually find a local accounting firm affiliated with one of the major international firms.

The preparation of consolidated financial statements, which are of very limited value if not audited, is less critical for bulk shipping operators than it is for liner operators. Nevertheless, it is definitely to be encouraged, and saves the prospective lender considerable work. Though consolidation may seem difficult if the only connecting links among the shipowning companies are common shareholders, lenders will still appreciate the work savings resulting from preparation of a consolidated statement on a pro-forma basis.

The second issue pertains to the valuation of the vessel collateral. Lenders vary somewhat in their approach to this subject. Some feel that they are relying for their credit judgment primarily on the value of the vessel. These lenders often, therefore, insist upon inspecting the vessel. Though few have competent engineers on their own staffs, there are any number of consultants that are willing to perform this service for a fee. Other lenders feel that they are relying primarily on the cash flow from operation of the vessel and the management capabilities of the owner and, therefore, do not require a physical inspection. They may, however, wish to inspect the classification society records.[3]

Regardless of their attitude toward physical inspections, lenders always need to estimate the value of their vessel collateral. This is a function traditionally performed by the sale and purchase shipbroking community. There are a few problems in this respect. First, there is some room for legitimate disagreement, particularly when it comes to specialized vessels for which there is no active sale and purchase market. Second, shipbrokers specialize to some degree, and hence may not be familiar with all types of tonnage. Their views on the value of an unfamiliar type of vessel may, therefore, not be reliable. Last (and sad to say), shipbrokers can sometimes be influenced. A lender should exercise great care when the valuing shipbroker is also an intermediary in the proposed vessel purchase, or even if the borrower is otherwise one of the shipbroker's valued clients. The lender should be particularly careful of valuations provided by the prospective borrower.

There is no complete answer to these problems. Legitimate disagreement can be handled by obtaining two or more valuations (not a bad idea in any case), and simply relying on the lowest figure obtained. The other two problems can only be handled by deliberately cultivating the shipbroking community so as to learn as much as possible about brokers' strengths and weaknesses with respect to specialities, and about their ongoing client bases. Ideally, a lender should try to turn one shipbroker into a "house" broker; i.e., one owing its primary loyalty to the lender in any given potential lender/client conflict of interest. Unfortunately, shipbrokers make a living from commissions on vessel sales rather than from valuation fees. Therefore, short of a generous retainer arrangement, the ideal situation may be impossible to achieve. However, in the long run, such a retainer usually proves to be worth its cost.

There is one other point worth noting about valuations, and that is that they represent an estimate of market value at a particular point in time.[4] Therefore, from a lender's perspective, it makes good policy to revalue the vessel on a regular basis (say quarterly, semi-annually, or annually). In fact, if the loan agreement contains a security maintenance clause,[5] such revaluations may be absolutely critical.

Bulk Shipping

In bulk shipping, transactions are done as quasi project financings: that is, it is intended that the vessel(s) involved will earn the funds needed for debt service. An owner, by choosing to mortgage a second ship, may subsidize the repayment of a loan taken out to finance the purchase of a first ship. This does not, however, change the essential nature of the transaction. The lender views the project as a total package: that is, if two or more ships are involved, the cash flow from operation of all the vessels is expected to be adequate to cover all operating costs and debt service. Thus, the heart of the analysis of a bulk ship financing is a cash flow forecast. This is simpler than it may sound.

The Cash Flow Forecast

The most difficult part of the cash flow forecast is apt to be the revenues. If the vessel is to be employed on a time charter for the full period of the loan, the relevant rate can be determined from the charter. Keeping in mind that charterhire is due only for days worked, one can reasonably estimate future revenues by calculating what would be due if the vessel were onhire 100% of the time, and then deducting a conservative allowance for offhire time relating to maintenance, repair, and other purposes. Fifteen days per year is quite a conservative allowance for a relatively modern ship, but one might wish to allow more for an older ship. The classification society records may shed light on the vessel's frequency of repair rate, and if the transaction is a refinancing, historical revenues under the time charter may also reveal historical offhire.

From the revenues, one can proceed to the costs. The first, usually deducted directly from the charterhire, is the brokerage commission. Usually the owner will reveal the actual commission rate, but 2-1/2% is a reasonably conservative assumption in the absence of actual data.

Operating costs, consisting mainly of crewing costs, maintenance, and insurance are slightly more problematical: the owner will normally be happy to provide an estimate on a per day basis, but this estimate is apt to err on the low side, and hence needs to be cross checked. One of the advantages of being a lender to multiple shipowners is that it is likely that another client will have similar vessels, and is thus in a position to provide comparative estimates. This can be arranged without breeching confidentiality. In the absence of such data, many shipbrokers maintain files of operating cost data, and may be willing to provide comparative figures. Once an acceptable starting figure has been determined, it is normal to apply an escalation factor for the years that follow. The choice of any specific escalation factor depends on inflationary expectations, and the degree to which cost increases are allowed for by way of related escalation of the time charter rate. For example, if inflation is running at 5% annually, and the time charter allows for rate escalation to cover 40% of the operating costs, one might actually project a 3% per annum operating cost escalation.

Under a typical time charter, the charterer is responsible for all voyage costs (see below), and hence these can be ignored.

Debt service (or lease payments as the case may be) can be assumed as per the agreement between the borrower and the lender. If the loan is subject to interest on a floating rate basis, it is necessary to make an assumption with respect to interest rates. It is prudent to do this conservatively (by, for instance, assuming that rates will be at the cap, if there is a cap), or better yet, by doing "what-if" analysis (see below) to determine the maximum level of interest the transaction can tolerate.

In most cases, one can safely ignore taxation. However, if the vessel's operations will be subject to income tax, one must determine the applicable depreciation rate, apply that rate to the purchase price to determine the actual depreciation charge, and deduct this charge as an additional expense. Taxable income will consist of the net result so far plus the principal payment.

To this figure must be applied the appropriate marginal corporate income tax rate (which will vary depending on the tax jurisdiction) to determine the tax payable.

The objective is to reach a net cash flow figure for the period (usually one year) in question. In a jurisdiction not subject to income tax, this figure will be the result of the deduction of brokerage, operating costs, and all debt service from charterhire revenues. In a jurisdiction subject to income tax, the relevant figure will be the same, but with the additional deduction of tax payable. It is important to note that depreciation as an expense is relevant only for the purpose of calculating taxation. It involves no outflow of cash, and therefore has no impact on cash flow. An example of a cash flow forecast is shown below as Figure 1. This analysis relates to the purchase of a 30,000 DWT products tanker built in 1977 for a price of U.S. $6 million. The vessel is to fly the Liberian flag using European officers and Chinese ratings, and is to be time chartered for the full period of the five year loan.

Figure 1

Cash Flow Forecast: 30,000 DWT Products Tanker

(000's: U.S. $)

Year	*1*	*2*	*3*	*4*	*5*
Charterhire[A]	2,760	2,760	2,760	3,105	3,105
-Brokerage[B]	69	69	69	78	78
Net Charterhire	2,691	2,691	2,691	3,027	3,027
Operating Costs[C]	1,460	1,534	1,611	1,693	1,778
Cash Flow Avail. for Debt Service	1,231	1,157	1,080	1,334	1,249
Total Debt Service[D]	1,114	1,114	1,114	1,114	1,114
Net Cash Flow	117	43	(34)	220	135
+ Beginning Cash[E]	500	617	660	626	846
Ending Cash	617	660	626	846	981

Assumptions

A. $8.00/DWT/month in years 1-3, and $10.00/DWT/month in years 4-5. 15 days offhire per year.
B. 2-1/2% of gross charterhire.
C. $4,000/day, 365 days/year. Inflation factor 8%, but time charter provides for escalation covering 40% of operating cost escalations. Escalation rate applied analytically is therefore 4.8%.
D. 70% finance ratio ($4.2 million loan), payable in ten level semi-annual payments with interest fixed for the full term at 11%.
E. Owner provides $500,000 at start for start-up costs and cash cushion.

A lender deriving the kind of result illustrated in Figure 1 would, assuming other, non-quantitative factors were acceptable (see further on), probably be inclined to look favorably on this proposed financing. However, it is worth noting that the projected cash surpluses are not particularly large. If the assumptions are sufficiently conservative, this should not be worrisome. It is also worth noting that as the charterer is responsible for all voyage costs (bunkers, port fees, canal fees, etc), and as charterhire under a time charter is normally paid monthly or semi-monthly in advance, working capital requirements are minimal. Likewise, start-up costs are typically limited to transportation of the crew to the vessel, insurance premiums, and victualling, which is not the case with spot market operations.

The foregoing transaction is relatively easy to assess on a quantitative basis, as the future revenue stream at least has the appearance of certainty (see the below discussion of non-quantitative risk factors). However, the situation is rather different in the absence of a time charter, or if a time charter expires before the final maturity of the loan.

There are two basic ways of approaching this problem. The first is the "typical voyage" analysis approach, and is particularly valid for a vessel trading under a contract of affreightment (COA). Under a COA, the charterer, cargo, and freight rate are known, and in many cases, the first two of these presuppose particular loading and discharging ports. Assuming this information is available, one can easily calculate the freight revenue for a single voyage, net of brokerage (if any).

The cost side of "typical voyage" analysis can also be easily calculated once certain information is available. This information is the length of the voyage (steaming time); port time (both loading and discharging); time steaming in ballast, if applicable; fuel and lubricant consumption, while steaming and while in port; the applicable port costs at both the loading and discharge ports; and any transit fees, canal fees, etc. that may be applicable in steaming from the loading port to the discharge port (including any ballast legs). Owners perform this kind of analysis all the time, and hence most of this information should be readily available.

By calculating operating costs as in the time charter example, but only for the period covering a single voyage; adding the other costs noted above; and deducting the total from the freight revenue, one can arrive at a voyage contribution figure. By manipulating the length of voyage data and making a reasonable allowance for offhire, one can determine the number of voyages per year that the vessel can make, and hence calculate a figure for cash flow available for debt service. The remaining calculations proceed as with time charter employment.

All these calculations are cumbersome, but not difficult. However, there remain two major problems. The first is that the "typical voyage" discussion so far has assumed that the vessel is employed under only one COA, and that this COA fully utilizes the vessel's capacity. Neither of these assumptions is necessarily valid. For example, though a tanker usually will have great difficulty finding a cargo to carry back to or close to its original loading port, a dry cargo vessel or combination carrier may not have the same problem.[6] It may, in fact, have another COA for the return voyage (or to an acceptably close port), but even without a COA, it may be possible to secure spot cargoes covering the return voyage.

If there is a COA for the return voyage, one can simply break each round voyage into two voyages, and repeat the previously described calculations for the return voyage. The sum of the two will then yield the desired figure for cash flow available for debt service. If, on the other hand, the vessel is employed in the spot market for the return voyages, there is no guarantee that there will be any cargo at all. The conservative analytical approach is to assume that such is the case. If the COA, on the assumption of a return voyage in ballast, is adequate to cover the debt service, then any return cargoes are simply additional cushion, or perhaps can be used to prepay debt under an "earnings recapture" clause.[7] If on the other hand, the COA is not adequate by itself to cover the debt service requirements, the only way to proceed is to independently assess the availability of return cargoes. This is difficult and risky unless the lender's ship financing business is at a volume that justifies having a dry cargo broker on its staff, or on a consulting basis with a retainer.

The second problem (aside from the cumbersome nature of the calculations) with "typical voyage" analysis is that COA's usually have a duration of twelve months or less. Thus, the analysis is vulnerable beyond the duration of the contract: the contract may not be renewed at all, and if it is renewed, it may be at a less favorable freight rate, or involve a smaller volume of cargo.

In some cases, a shipowner may be able to demonstrate that a particular COA, despite its stated limited duration is, in fact, "evergreen": that is, it is continually renewed because of the ongoing transportation requirements of the charterer. When this is so, many analysts continue to use the "typical voyage" approach, but assume that the rates beyond the duration of the present contract will be subject to some reasonable escalation rate. They also apply an escalation rate to the costs.

This is actually a very misleading approach, as economically speaking, the COA rate is going to be governed to some degree by the current freight market. That is, a charterer's willingness to pay a premium rate in order to ensure the availability of transportation is going to be limited by the open market alternatives. If the charterer fails to ship the volume called for in the contract, there is little, as a practical matter, that the owner can do about it. He is, therefore, forced to accept rates having some relationship to the current market, and the market, unfortunately, does not move ever upward.[8]

A more useful analytical approach is to back into the problem by calculating breakeven rates (this is really the only approach to use with pure spot market operations, and may also be applied to the later years of contract of affreightment employment). This approach makes a simplifying assumption that appears to be reasonable in real life: that the difference between spo rates and voyage time charter rates at any given point in time is the voyag costs. These costs include, mainly, bunkers (fuel), canal/transit fees, an port costs: i.e., those costs that can be calculated only for a particular voyage as distinguished from those applicable to ongoing operations (manning costs maintenance, and insurance, for instance). This observation about th relationship between spot rates and voyage time charter rates permits on to ignore voyage costs with a reasonable degree of safety. One can, therefore add the debt service and the daily operating cost as in Figure 1 to determin the revenue required in order to breakeven cash flow wise. This figure (o rather one for each year) can then be translated, making an offhire allowance into a time charter rate which can be compared to historical current, an projected time charter rates in order to assess its achievability.

This approach has one obvious drawback: it does not actually allow one t project whether the cash flow will be adequate for debt service. However it does allow one to assess how far the market can move before cash flov becomes inadequate. Knowing this makes it easier to monitor a loan on a ongoing basis. It may even be possible to insert a clause in a loan agreemen requiring an owner to cover his market risk by fixing the vessel on a perio charter or by buying freight rate futures contracts,[9] when freight rates o futures reach a specified level.

There is also one other observation that should be borne in mind whe considering a transaction involving spot market employment. When con sidering a transaction involving a medium term time charter, as in Figur 1, it was noted that because time charterhire is normally paid in advance working capital requirements are minimal. This is not necessarily true wit spot market or COA operations because in some cases, charterhire is no paid in advance, and because the owner must fund the voyage costs (whic are substantial) even though he recovers them in the freight rate Unfortunately, the only way to allow for this in advance is to require a highe level of starting liquidity.

When considering bulk shipping transactions, especially in spot market cases it is useful to engage in what-if analysis. What-if analysis refers to the proces of changing the assumptions in the cash flow model described in this chapte in order to test the impact of these changes on the results. Going throug this process can indicate where the transaction is vulnerable, and increas one's understanding of the risks. Though the calculations may appea cumbersome, the model can be very neatly set up in a personal compute using any standard spreadsheet program, making the what-if analysis proces quite simple.[10]

The choice of an appropriate finance ratio depends largely on the results of ash flow analysis. Other things being equal, the greater the perceived risk, he lower the finance ratio. The perceived risk depends heavily on how xposed the vessel will be to market risk. Many lenders have expressed the iew that they will not take market risk, and hence always insist on period ime charter employment. Such time charters do give at least the illusion of ertainty about the vessel's earnings, but for reasons discussed further on, his certainty is usually overrated. Nevertheless, lenders will typically be more enerous when the transaction contains an element of fixed employment, elatively less generous when there is a COA, and least generous when perations will be on a purely spot basis.

The specific ratio is a matter of negotiation between shipowner and lender. n theory, the maximum ratio should be that ratio that results in an amount f debt that can be serviced from the conservatively projected cash flow. Historically, finance ratios have generally ranged from 50% to 100%, depending on the degree of exposure to market risk. Ratios as generous as hese have become very rare in the last few years, 50% to 70% now being nore normal. This may turn out to be an overreaction. Even with a spot narket operation, there are situations which can justify higher ratios if one s confident about one's understanding of the market. However, this resupposes that a lender is willing to take market risk, and that he believes e is being adequately paid for that risk in the transaction pricing. It is also vorth noting that timing plays a role here. High finance ratios are less risky vhen ship values are depressed, and lenders would be well advised to allow ower ratios when values are buoyant. Ironically, the reverse is more ormal.[11]

Parenthetically, it should be noted that the foregoing should be interpreted n light of what other security may be offered. Apart from other vessels, vhose value can be at least guessed at, this usually means the shipowner's ersonal guarantee. The assessment of these guarantees will be discussed urther on, but as a practical matter, its value depends heavily on the degree f leverage and the employment prospects for the other vessels in his fleet. A strong guarantee viewed in these terms might justify accepting a relatively igh finance ratio even in a spot transaction, if the remainder of the fleet ad a low ratio and relatively secure employment. This becomes a judgmental ssue for which there are no simple rules.

Operating Risks

The discussion so far has centered on the analysis and projection of financial i.e., quantifiable) results. There are also a number of unquantifiable aspects to the analysis of bulk ship financing transactions, though these will inevitably have an impact on the financial results.

With the exception of financings involving vessels employed on bareboat charters, ship financings involve operating risks in addition to market risks. The first of these pertains to the rather obvious concern with the moral reputation and financial condition of charterers. This concern escalates geometrically with the length of term of the charter. With a voyage charter, the risk is very limited: only from the date of fixture to the date of payment (usually the same as the date of loading). Likewise, the vessel's master need not release the bill of lading until the charterhire has been paid, and the resulting control over the cargo gives the owner considerable leverage over the shipper, who in turn has considerable incentive to make timely payment. Collection of amounts due later such as demurrage may be more difficult, but usually the amounts are relatively small.

The problem is somewhat different when a time charter involving more than one payment period is involved. If a payment is delayed for whatever reason (even if due to bank error), the odds are that a voyage will be in progress, and thus the owner runs the risk that in addition to going unpaid, it will incur the costs of completing the voyage. Likewise, the longer the term of the charter, the greater the owner's exposure to market risk if the charterer becomes financially insolvent before the charter expires. The owner's bankers can be a great assistance in checking on the reputation of prospective charterers, and it is in the bankers' interest to be helpful. When longer term charters are involved, the risk assessment process should also include an analysis of the financial condition of the charterer. The financing bank should be in a position to do this; otherwise, it should abstain. Particular care should be taken with credit decisions made on a ''name'' basis (i.e., strictly on the basis of general reputation, without financial analysis). For example, many owners (and banks) incurred losses as the result of relying on the good name of such charterers as Sanko Steamship, Salen, and Irish Shipping, all of which are now bankrupt.

Extra special care must be taken when doing business with so-called time charter operators. Most of these operators employ vessels on time charters, and use them to carry spot cargoes, making their profits in the spread between the spot and time charter rates. This can work as long as the time charter equivalents[12] of the spot rates equal or exceed the rates at which the vessels were chartered in. However, in a rising market, the temptation is to invest profits in new time charters. When the market turns down, which it always does eventually, the previous profits turn very quickly into losses.[13] Furthermore, these companies very seldom have much financial substance. Many owners, and presumably bankers as well, incurred major losses with the bankruptcy of Clover Trading in 1981, and this is far from an isolated case. Unless these time charter operators commit forward for only a limited period, or have firm medium term cargo commitments that can be relied upon, dealing with them on anything but a short-term basis is very risky.

Furthermore, the apparent comfort associated with a medium term charter is often illusory. First, unless the charter contains provisions for escalation of the rate to cover increases in operating costs, the owner can be squeezed between the freight rate and inflationary forces that were not predictable at the time the charter was signed. As a result of the inflation of the 1970's, most medium term charters now include cost escalation provisions, but experience suggests that with the much reduced inflation of the 1980's (particularly in U.S. dollar terms), and the increased competitiveness of the depressed markets, this tendency may be allowed to lapse.

In addition to the possibility of a cost squeeze, there is another problem associated with medium term charters. This is the tendency of many charterers that signed charters when rates were high to pressure the owners for a reduction in rates when the market weakens. In most cases, the weak market leaves the owner no alternative but to comply.[14]

There is little a lender can do about this, but it behooves it well to review such charters thoroughly, particularly with respect to escalation and cancellation provisions.

The second category of operating risk is the operating competence of the manager. This is true whether the manager is the owner or a third party.[15] The proposition is very simple, but surprisingly often ignored: a vessel not operating earns no hire. Further, a vessel quickly develops an unfavorable reputation if it is unable to meet its obligations under its charters, thus, at best, forcing it to accept below market freight rates, or at worst, resulting in legitimate charter cancellations.

As noted previously, if the vessel being financed has a track record under the same management, some insight into operating competence can be gained by examining its offhire record. This cannot be done, of course, with the purchase of a new vessel or of a second-hand vessel previously under other management, although the same insight may be gained by examining the operating track record of other vessels under the same management. Financial information is of limited use in this respect, and often unavailable. Indeed, the principal source of this information is general market contacts, particularly the shipbroking community, but also the agency sector, and where possible, shippers.

It is worth noting also that there may be a circular relationship amon financial condition, the condition of vessels, and operating record. An owne that is financially weak, either because he is undercapitalized, or as the resul of a weak market, will tend to defer discretionary costs, particularly in th maintenance sector. This is apt, especially with older vessels, to eventuall have an adverse impact on the operating track record, which in turn is ap to have an adverse impact on the vessel's earnings. The cycle can start a any of the three points.

Legal Risks

In addition to assessment of financial condition, market risk, and operatin risk, there are a number of other factors that both owner and lender nee to consider when evaluating any given transaction. The first of these factor falls in the general category of legal risks. These in turn fall broadly int two categories: rules of the flag, and law and jurisdiction.

From a financing perspective, one of the primary relevant rules of the fla is that pertaining to ease of registration and enforcement of the mortgage With the exception of the flags of convenience, most mortgages must b registered in their home countries. Since most vessels subject to suc mortgages are also subject to nationality of ownership requirements, this i sometimes a bit awkward, but not a major difficulty for an internationa lender to surmount. More important considerations are whether th underlying body of law recognizes the peculiar nature of the maritim mortgage; whether the agency for the registration of the mortgage is speedil and inexpensively accessible; and whether it is recognized as valid by (an hence enforceable in) legal jurisdictions other than the home country.

Another relevant consideration is whether the body of law and/o governmental regulation puts serious obstacles in the way of sale of the vess in the international market. Given that the local market may not be ver active, it is important to the lender that it be able to speedily de-register th vessel so that it can be sold elsewhere.

A detailed survey of the various ship mortgages is not within the scope o this book. Generally speaking, however, experienced ship financiers fee comfortable with the mortgages available under the major flags o convenience (Liberia, Panama, Vanuatu, etc.); those available under the flag of the major maritime nations, such as the Netherlands, Norway, Greece the U.S., and England; and those available under the flags of various presen or former Commonwealth nations whose legal structure is patterned afte the laws of England (Bermuda, the Bahamas, Hong Kong, Singapore anada, Cyprus, etc.). The mortgages available in jurisdictions whose legal asis is the Napoleonic Code (France and Italy, for instance) are more ontroversial. Some countries, particularly in Africa (excluding Liberia and outh Africa), the Middle East (excluding Sharjah), and Latin America have o marine mortgage law to speak of, and foreign lenders usually avoid them. Iowever, within Latin America, Brazil appears to be an exception, as its nortgage law seems to meet international standards, and its de-registration rovisions not to be onerous. Others, such as Argentina and Chile have easonably sophisticated, thought somewhat cumbersome ship mortgage laws, ut onerous restrictions on de-registration. Lenders are divided in their pinions of these. A lender considering a transaction involving an unfamiliar lag is well advised to consult with experienced legal counsel, especially if he country involved is not one of the generally accepted ones. Even the U.S. nortgage has its problems,[16] especially for non-U.S. banks.[17]

he rules of the flag discussed so far are risks of a legal nature. Other rules f the flag are risks (or opportunities) whose impact is primarily economic. or example, most national flags (as distinguished from flags of convenience) equire that at least a portion of the crew be nationals of the flag country. hey often go so far as to dictate wages and social benefits, and even in eveloping and semi-industrialized countries, these are not necessarily cheap. gain, some countries require that insurance be arranged through government ntities. Even though most of this insurance is re-insured in the international narket and, therefore, may be acceptable cover (see the discussion below bout assignments of insurance), the premiums are apt to be artificially high. astly, national flag carriers are often highly regulated in ways that do not lways make economic sense. Brazilian shipowners, for instance, are largely oreclosed from cross trading. The problem is not limited to developing ountries, though. One of the major difficulties facing the lines based in the J.S. has been that regulations, usually accompanying acceptance of subsidies, ave forced owners to continue to provide certain levels of service on specified rades even when the trades have become uneconomic. The point here is that t behooves a lender to understand its prospective borrower's regulatory nvironment.

y the same token, the rules of the flag may represent, or appear to represent pportunities. For example, many governments, in an effort to develop ational flag fleets, have made operating cost and/or construction cost ubsidies available. Some have made available advantageous financing chemes. Others, principally oil exporting countries, have discounted the price f bunkers to somewhere near their cost (i.e., well below what used to be he world market price).[18] In addition, most national flags (including those f the developed countries) practice some sort of cargo reservation or reference.

Sometimes viable ventures can be based on such subsidies, and this subject will be discussed further in Chapter IX. However, it is important to consider one cautionary note. These subsidies are political in nature and, therefore, by definition transitory, and sometimes lacking in substance. For example, it is the Reagan administration's lack of enthusiasm for subsidies that has forced U.S. shipowners to adjust to financing on commercial terms. By the same token, the repeal of Chilean coastal cargo reservation forced a number of Chilean flag operators to reflag in Panama in order to remain competitive. For another example, many cargo reservation policies are subject to quotation of market rates, which definitely limits their economic value. Likewise, if there are no cargoes or import and export cargoes are grossly out of balance as the result of balance of trade issues, the value of cargo reservation policies is further limited. In addition, many subsidies are a two-edged sword. They are accompanied by requirements that often eventually turn out to be uneconomic.

The point is that it also behooves a lender to understand its borrower's political environment, and its place within that environment.[19] Alternatively, a lender may not unreasonably take the view that it does not wish to take these legal and political risks of the flag, and instead finance only projects with a strong economic basis. This would probably be an overreaction. However, it is no accident that two of the largest flags in the world in terms of registered tonnage are Liberia and Panama, both flags of convenience, under which no subsidies are available. It is also interesting to note that owners from developing countries[20] are surprisingly well represented under these flags.

Law and jurisdiction is a rather different issue from the rules of the flag. Law and jurisdiction refers to the body of law governing all the financing documentation other than the mortgage, and the venue in which it is to be enforced. In most cases, the law and jurisdiction is chosen by the lender, though occasionally the borrower's central bank or finance ministry exerts pressure towards to the use of its law. In addition, a bank doing business through its branch in another country may feel compelled to use the law of that country.[21] The decision to do so is no better or worse than the decision to have a branch in that country. Ship financing done through banks' offshore branches (such as those established as a matter of tax convenience on various Caribbean islands) are usually governed by the laws and courts of England or the laws and courts of the State of New York. In fact, these two bodies of law generally dominate ship financing, although this may merely reflect the dominance of U.S. and English banks in this market sector. Overall, law and jurisdiction is not usually a controversial issue, and any doubts can be fairly easily resolved by consultation with internationally experienced legal counsel. However, most experienced ship financiers insist that the financing documents specify that the law and jurisdiction is non-exclusive. This provides the flexibility to enforce the agreement elsewhere if circumstances warrant, which may well be the case with vessels operating internationally.

The Assignment of Earnings

The key to the success of the bulk ship financing transaction is, contrary to popular belief, not simply the value of the asset financed. The sale of the vessel is actually the secondary source of repayment much sought after by all lenders. The primary source of repayment will always be the vessel's earnings. Consequently, successful ship financiers pay very close attention to their control of the earnings stream. Legally speaking, this control is accomplished by way of the assignment of earnings. The assignment can be in either of two forms: a specific assignment of earnings if the vessel is to be employed on a medium term time charter; or a general assignment of earnings, under which the owner agrees to pledge all future earnings of the vessel, and to execute specific assignments if, in the future, the vessel is employed under a time charter for in excess of a specified term mutually agreed to by the owner and the lender. The assignment of earnings can, in theory, be incorporated in the loan agreement, but most experienced ship finance attorneys recommend that it be a separate document.

The easiest earnings flow to control is that from a medium term time charter. The assignment of the charter specifies a bank account to which charterhire is to be paid, and this account is typically under the exclusive control of and pledged to the lender. The assignment and the payment instructions are notified to the charterer, who acknowledges receipt. Charterhire is then received into that account in accordance with the terms of the charter, usually monthly or semi-monthly, and as long as the financing is not in default, the lender, after withholding a pro rata share of the next payment of principal and interest (this pro rata share is typically invested at interest until the next payment date), passes the funds on to an operating account under the shipowner's control, from which they can be used to pay operating expenses.

There are four primary possible difficulties with the arrangement. First, it is possible that as a result of substandard performance, the charterhire will be insufficient to cover operating costs and debt service. This is one of the operating risks previously discussed. Second, the charter may provide for the charterer to deduct penalties for substandard performance from the gross charterhire (rather than paying the gross charterhire and having the owner remit the penalties back) with the same effect as above. The lender should make itself aware in advance of any such provisions. Third, as the result of a dispute between the owner and the charterer, the charterer may withhold payment of disputed amounts even though the charter makes no provision for doing so. The lender is protected somewhat in this instance if the charter assignment has been properly notified to and duly acknowledged by the charterer. Last, the charterer may either deliberately or inadvertently fail to cooperate in the assignment. The most common error would be for the charterer to pay the hire to an account controlled by the owner rather than to an account controlled by the lender. If the assignment was duly acknowledged, the charterer can be held legally responsible for this error, although it is often not politic or necessary to enforce this responsibility. Funds inadvertently released to the owner in this manner become subject to a provision in most assignment agreements that requires the owner to hold them in trust for the lender. Unfortunately, it is almost impossible to enforce involuntary compliance with this provision.

For charters of less than six to twelve months duration, the mechanics described above are rather cumbersome. Furthermore, if the vessel is employed under spot charters, voyage time charters, or contracts of affreightment, the timing and amounts of incoming payments are likely to be irregular. While it is still appropriate to require that payments be made to an account controlled by the lender, this arrangement is very vulnerable to charterer error. In addition, while it is possible to require that an owner specify that account in the payment provisions of its charters, it is very difficult to get charterers to acknowledge notice of assignment. Lastly, when incoming payments are irregular, the calculation of pro rata shares of the next principal and interest payments is awkward at best.

There is no fully satisfactory answer to these problems, but assuming an honorable and competent borrower, most experienced shipping bankers simply agree that as long as the financing is not in default, charterhire received will be passed automatically to the operating account.

To keep things in perspective, lenders should bear in mind that the value of an assigned charter may be rather limited. Though it is theoretically possible for a vessel to continue operating after an event of default, operations are likely to become increasingly difficult, especially if the lender decides not to release any funds for operating expenses. At this stage, the probability that the vessel will be arrested by the lender or by other creditors increases geometrically. Once the vessel has been arrested, the value of the assigned earnings is limited to the balance in the account under the lender's control.

There is one other possible situation that is of interest in the context of earnings assignments. This is the situation in which cargo transportation contracts run in favor of a parent company, with the actual transportation service being provided by one-ship-owning-subsidiaries. Some people have argued that as long as the parent company guarantees the subsidiary's vessel financing, it is redundant and unnecessary to also have an assignment of any charter between the parent and the subsidiary.

This redundancy is more apparent than real. Apart from the fact that it is a useful discipline to have the hire payments flow through a lender controlled account, the flow of funds through the parent company may relate to vessels other than the vessel financed. It is very helpful, with view to possible future legal enforcement, to isolate a flow of funds related directly to the financed vessel and lay a legally enforceable claim to it. This can best be accomplished by assignment of the charter. It is in this sense that the charter assignment is regarded as prime security, and is worth having even though there is a parent company guarantee.

Insurance Issues

The value of vessel collateral is dependent on the vessel's being in satisfactory operating condition, as otherwise it is useless to a prospective buyer. It should, therefore, be obvious that a lender would want to ensure that the vessel is adequately insured against damage and/or loss, and that this insurance is assigned in the lender's favor. By the same token, one can envisage situations in which as the result of vessel operations, an owner becomes responsible for liabilities that result in claims or liens that inhibit movement of the vessel, and perhaps are held by courts to rank ahead of the mortgage. Hence, a lender also would want to ensure that there is adequate liability insurance, and that this insurance is also assigned in the lender's favor.

Like the assignment of earnings, the assignment of insurance can, in theory, be incorporated in the loan agreement. However, experienced ship financing attorneys usually recommend that it be a separate document. The document itself is quite straightforward. The actual levels and types of insurance required are usually specified in detail in the mortgage, which may be incorporated by reference. The essence of the assignment agreement is a covenant by the shipowner to insure the vessel to the lender's satisfaction with underwriters acceptable to the lender; to give notice of the assignment to the underwriters and brokers; to have the lender named as loss payee in all insurance policies; to arrange for the underwriters, or in some cases, the insurance broker,[22] to acknowledge the assignment, confirm the naming of the lender as loss payee, and agree to give the lender notice of non-payment of premiums, and cancellation or non-renewal of policies; and to provide copies of all relevant policies and cover notes.

The assignment documents themselves are seldom controversial. The insurance requirements may be. The normal practice is to require that the hull and machinery insurance be between 110% and 130% of the loan amount,[23] the specific percentage being a negotiating point between the borrower and the lender. Likewise, it is normal practice to limit the maximum deductible, usually to $100,000, $250,000 or $500,000 depending on the lender's perception of the financial strength of the borrower. Lastly, the lender and the borrower typically agree that claims below some specified dollar amount may be paid directly to the owner instead of to the lender as loss payee. This practice is designed to minimize the need for administrative handling of the payment of small claims.

A much more difficult issue is the quality of insurance cover. Marine insurance risks are usually syndicated, which means that there is a multiplicity of underwriters to be evaluated. When one realizes that probably in excess of twenty percent of the property and casualty insurance companies in the United States are on the watch lists of their respective regulatory authorities, one quickly realizes how critical the question is. The dimensions of the problem rise dramatically when one realizes how difficult it is to assess the financial strength of an insurance underwriter. As one example only, a significant portion of the statutory financial statement of a U.S. based property and casualty company is a listing of its reinsurance arrangements. The dollar exposure to these other companies is enormous, and large losses have been incurred in this area. Professionals in the field employ staffs of accountants and actuaries to assess these companies, and it is usually unrealistic to expect banks[24] and owners to be appropriately equipped in-house.

Ship financing banks have traditionally addressed this problem by requiring the owner to provide at the closing a written opinion from his insurance broker that the insurance cover is adequate and appropriate for the vessel in question, and that the cover has been placed with underwriters of acceptable quality. Such opinions are largely useless. First, it is not realistic to expect to hold a broker legally responsible for its failure to foresee the failure of an underwriter. Second, the owner's broker has an obvious conflict of interest. The lender is far better served by employing a consultant (who may also be a broker) beholden only to the lender. The additional comfort is well worth the relatively small additional cost.

The evaluation of liability coverage is less of a problem. This coverage is usually provided by protection and indemnity associations (so-called P & I clubs). The P & I clubs are mutual associations of (primarily) shipowners that have the right to call on their members for aditional capital. They seldom get into major financial difficulties. Nevertheless, it is useful to have the consultant express an opinion on these as well.

Some lenders feel strongly that they must require mortgagee's interest insurance. This form of insurance covers the rather limited risk that a vessel's hull and machinery underwriters will refuse to pay claims on the grounds of fraud or gross negligence on the part of the owner. It is a situation that is likely to occur only in the event of a total loss, and as noted previously, fraud or gross negligence in a total loss situation is very difficult to prove. The insurance, which is typically taken out by the lender (at the borrower's expense) in an amount equal to the hull and machinery cover, is inexpensive. It is probably better to have it than not to have it, but on the whole it seems rather overrated, and lenders tend to expect far too much from it.[25]

Assuming that the lender and the borrower agree that there will be mortgagee's interest insurance, it is worth noting that the standard form is deficient in at least one major respect. The hull and machinery underwriters' refusal to pay on the grounds of fraud (for instance: they claim that the vessel was deliberately scuttled) is virtually certain to be subject to litigation. This litigation may take a long time (years even). The mortgagee's interest insurance claim will usually not be paid until this litigation has been decided by the courts. In the meantime, the loan remains outstanding, with interest accruing (and presumably unpaid) at the default rate which is very high. Thus, if and when the mortgagee's interest insurance claim is paid, it may well be insufficient to cover the full amount due.

It is possible to solve this problem by arranging for a policy that pays the claim at the time that the hull and machinery underwriters refuse to pay, but subject to recovery if the underwriters are subsequently forced by legal action to pay. Alternatively, the amount of the claim can be paid, at the time of refusal to pay by the hull and machinery underwriters, into an interest bearing escrow account that is then released if and when the courts rule in favor of the underwriters. This change in structure has precedent, and costs only a little additional. However, it will not be done unless the lender specifically so arranges through its own insurance broker.

Another recurring issue relating to insurance coverage is captive insurance companies. Captive insurance companies arose as a result of the difference between the retail (i.e., as quoted by underwriters to owners) and wholesale (i.e., as quoted by reinsurers to underwriters) premiums for insurance cover. By setting up an owner-controlled company to underwrite the owner's insurance cover, and reinsuring all of that cover in excess of applicable deductibles, owners can (once they have achieved sufficient volume to justify whatever minimum capital requirement is imposed by the relevant regulatory authority) realize a very meaningful cost savings.

From the lender's perspective, the difficulty is twofold. First, these offshore companies are usually capitalized at the minimum level required by law, and hence are not good risks in their own right. Second, since the borrower and the insurance company are under the same effective control, the lender runs the risk that the claims payments from the reinsurers to the captive will not flow to the lender as was contemplated by the assignment agreement.

Captive insurance operations usually add real economic value to the shipowning group taken as a whole, and hence it is normally not in the lender's interest to obstruct them. The usual way to surmount the two difficulties is to require assignment of the reinsurance.[26] Properly documented with appropriate notices to the reinsurers, this arrangement should normally be an acceptable risk.

Corporate Guarantees

Most ship financing transactions include at least one guarantee,[27] depending on the structure of the shipowning group. When the group is structured on a holding company basis as in Figure 2, it is normal for the transaction to be guaranteed by the holding company. This not only gives the lender additional security, but also partially compensates the lender for the risk that the borrowing company will be drained of liquidity to support other companies in the group that are operating in deficit.

Conventional financial statement analysis may be of some use in assessing the value of this guarantee if the holding company is in a position to make consolidated financial statements available. If one can adjust the accounting valuation of the fleet on the balance sheet to market value, one can get a very good picture of the owner's overall leverage. This can only be done by obtaining shipbroker valuations of all the vessels, and adjusting the stockholders' equity upward or downward to reflect the difference between market and accounting values. The leverage factor is then simply the fleet finance ratio, or the ratio of the total debt outstanding to the market value of the fleet.

Analysis of profit and loss statements is rather more problematical. These statements are usually prepared on an accrual basis, which means that they may not reflect the true cash results. Furthermore, analysis of past results can be a very poor guide to the future, as future results will depend mainly on the general market and the composition and employment profile of the fleet. Lastly, though the larger the fleet the less the impact on operating results of vessels added to or deleted from the fleet, the lender's lien will be only on the cash flow of the vessels in the security package. The remaining cash flow may be assigned to other lenders, and thus the value of a corporate guarantee assessed in terms of the profit and loss statement may be more apparent than real.

Rather more useful, however, is the historical analysis of the statement of changes in financial position (sometimes known as sources and uses of funds analysis). This can result in a succinct picture of the shipowner's investment

Figure 2

Typical Holding Company Structure

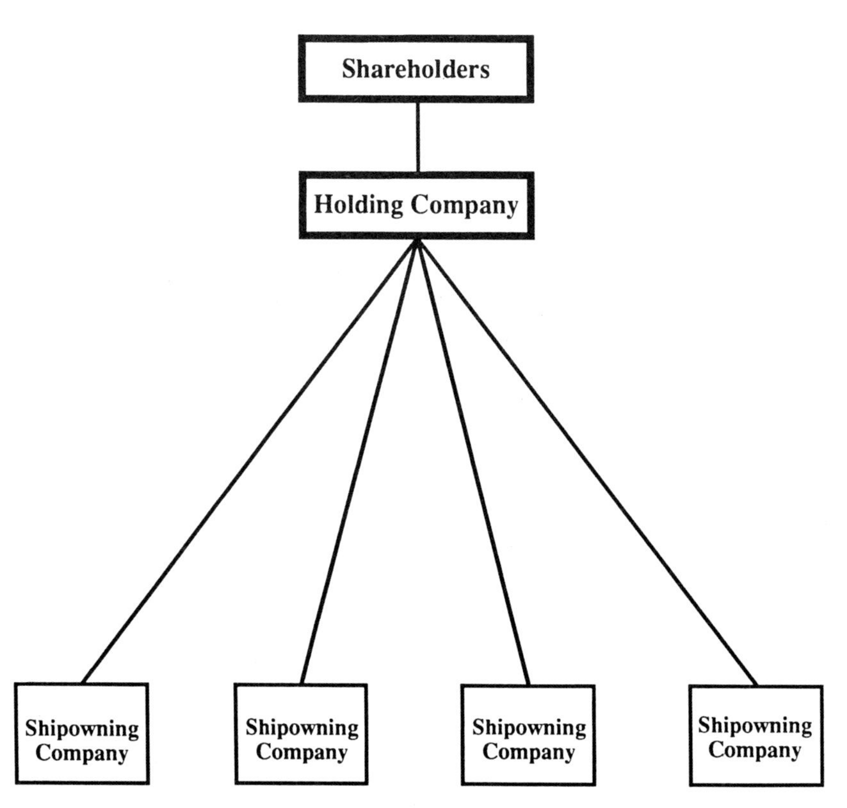

Share Ownership

and financing decisions in the recent past. By evaluating ship sale and purchase decisions in relation to the movements in the general market, and by assessing the amounts and terms of financing arrangements, one can get a very clear view of successes and failures in these respects. Indeed, owners can also find this type of analysis useful.[28]

Properly prepared audit reports include sources and uses of funds analysis usually under the label of "Statement of Changes in Financial Position", "Statement of Sources and Uses of Funds", or "Statement of Sources and Uses of Cash". Unfortunately, the accounting profession has not agreed on standards for the preparation and presentation of these statements and, therefore, they differ considerably from one to another. Likewise they vary in usefulness. The most important information, however, is usually there if the lender (or owner) knows what to look for. Even if such a statement is lacking, it is possible, by manipulation of profit and loss statements and balance sheet figures to derive a reasonable approximation.

Figure 3 is an example of sources and uses of funds analysis, but a few explanations will make it more useful.

First, the concept of depreciation as a non-cash expense (or a "source" of funds) is probably more familiar to lenders and bankers than to owners. Depreciation is the result of the matching principle of accounting: an asset acquired, such as a ship, will generate revenue for more than one accounting period and, therefore, to charge the entire vessel acquisition cost as an expense in the acquisition period would grossly understate profitability in that period, and overstate profitability in future periods. In order to more appropriately match revenues with expenses, the accounting convention is to "capitalize" the acquisition costs as an asset on the balance sheet, and to amortize these accumulated costs over the useful (i.e., revenue generating) life of the asset by charging an expense against revenues. However, this expense, representing as it does cash outlays incurred in a prior accounting period, does not itself represent an outlay of cash. Therefore, this expense does not represent a financing requirement, and accordingly may be regarded conceptually as an addition to profits or an offset to losses.

Figure 3

The XXX Shipping Group (Consolidated)
Statement of Changes in Financial Position

(millions: U.S. $)

Period	1/01/84 – 12/31/84	1/01/85 – 12/31/85	1/01/86 – 12/31/86	Total
Net Profit	–2.0	–2.5	1.0	– 3.5
Depreciation	1.0	1.0	2.0	4.0
Funds from Operations	–1.0	–1.5	3.0	.5
Change: Net Working Investment	– .5	– .5	– .5	– 1.5
Capital Expenditures	–3.0	—	5.0	2.0
Investments/Advances Affiliates	.5	.5	1.0	2.0
Debt Repayment	3.0	2.5	2.5	8.0
Total Uses of Funds	—	2.5	8.0	10.5
Financing Requirements	1.0	4.0	5.0	10.0
New Term Debt	—	—	3.0	3.0
New Short Term Debt	—	—	—	—
New Equity	—	2.0	2.0	4.0
Change in Liquidity Reserve	–1.0	–2.0	—	3.0
Total Financing	1.0	4.0	5.0	10.0

A similar line of reasoning applies to certain other "non-cash" expenses that sometimes appear in financial statements. These expenses plus depreciation, when added back to profits, yield a funds from operations figure representing the contribution (or lack thereof) of business operations to the funding requirements of the business.

Net working investment[29] may be a new concept to both lenders and borrowers, and is rather different from the more usual concept of net working capital. The latter is simply the difference between the value of those assets convertible to cash within one year (current assets), and those obligations due to be paid within one year (current liabilities).[30] Net working capital, and certain other analyticai tools such as the current ratio (ratio of current assets to current liabilities) and the acid-test or quick ratio (ratio of current assets less inventory to current liabilities), are widely used measures of a business' short term liquidity. Because they also reflect the results of cash management and financing decisions, they unfortunately result in distortions, particularly when (as in bulk shipping) net working investment requirements are typically negative.

Net working investment is the difference between all current assets, excluding cash and temporary investments (otherwise known as the liquidity reserve), and all current liabilities, excluding any obligations for borrowed money. The resulting figure indicates the net requirement for assets (apart from vessels) needed to conduct the business on an ongoing basis. In the bulk shipping business, charterhire is typically paid in advance, and consequently there is no need to extend credit and build up accounts receivable. In fact, most receivables in bulk shipping companies reflect non-operating items due, such as insurance claims. Likewise, as bulk shipping companies are really service companies rather than manufacturers, distributors, or retailers of goods, they have no true inventory requirements. Inventory accounts, when they appear at all, tend to consist of spare parts, and sometimes fuel. The ongoing current asset requirements, therefore, tend to be minimal.

On the other hand, the non-borrowed current liability accounts tend to be substantial. First, shipowners tend to purchase bunkers on credit terms of thirty to sixty days.[31] As bunkers are the single largest cost, the amount may be quite large. Second, the owner is usually able to accrue crew wages for some period of time. The result is that the non-borrowed current liability accounts tend to exceed the ongoing current asset requirements and, therefore, net working investment is negative, or in other words, a source of funds. An interesting corollary is that as the fleet grows, this source of funds also grows, and vice versa. This pattern is exactly the reverse of most lines of business.

The figure for capital expenditures (a negative figure represents the sale of assets, a source of funds) is usually available in the audit report. However, if for some reason it is not available, one can calculate the net (i.e., net of fixed asset sales) capital expenditures by using the following formula:

$$CE_2 = NFA_2 + Dep_2 - NFA_1$$

where CE = capital expenditures; NFA = net fixed assets (subscript 2 refers to the current year, subscript 1 to the immediately preceding year); and Dep. refers to depreciation expense.

Investments and advances to affiliates should be considered as similar to capital expenditures. Usually they represent less than majority ownership of single purpose shipowning companies, and hence involve similar risks.

The remaining categories in the statement should be self-explanatory. However, it is worth noting that only by examination of the figures for multiple years can one see patterns. Likewise, totals across the years may be useful. Since vessel purchases are the main capital burden, and the market is cyclical, related capital expenditures tend to vary widely from year to year. Sometimes a vessel acquisition program is executed over multiple accounting periods, which makes aggregate figures more useful in understanding what is going on.

The foregoing analysis of the balance sheet and historical sources and uses of funds gives some insight into the overall financial structure of the business, and into historical patterns of investment and financing decisions. It does not, however, answer the critical question of how much debt is too much, or, in other words, whether the group as a whole will be able to service its obligations (see Fleet Cash Flow Analysis below).

Personal Guarantees

When the shares of individual shipowning companies are held directly by one or more individuals rather than by a holding company, and even if they are owned by a holding company that is itself directly owned by individuals understood to have financial substance apart from the vessels controlled by the holding company, the normal practice is for the individual(s) to personally guarantee the borrowings in order to link the business operations together.

There are three obvious, but surprisingly often ignored, qualitative considerations with respect to personal guarantees. First, there is no excuse for a lender's doing business with an owner known in advance to be selective in his willingness to honor his obligations. Some lenders apparently believe that the secured nature of the transaction gives them protection from a dishonest owner. One simple example should suffice to put an end to this illusion. If a ship undergoes repairs, the lender may see the payment flow through the vessel operating account. He may not see that the shipyard on-remits a portion of that payment to the owner's personal account in

Switzerland. The heart of the transaction is double invoicing, and there are many opportunities for this kind of abuse that a lender has no way of controlling.

The second and slightly more subtle issue is that adversity is the only real test of an owner's character. The industry is full of examples of owners that had an absolutely clean record until, as a result of investment errors and/or depressed market conditions, they came under financial pressure. Sometimes under these circumstances otherwise honest people become dishonest in an attempt to avoid losing a previously earned fortune. Although it is not foolproof, a track record long enough to include at least one set of very adverse circumstances results in greater confidence about character judgments. Owners having less of a track record should be perceived as involving greater risk and, therefore, the rewards related to the transaction should be greater.

There is, however, a hidden trap in relying on the long, favorable moral track record of a shipowning group. If it is a public company, a management shift, particularly at the top of the hierarchy, may make that track record no longer relevant: almost as if the track record were to start over again. With private, family controlled groups, the issue is particularly difficult. If the track record of the group is long enough that the management is passing to a new generation, it is dangerous to assume that the new generation will abide by the values of the old. One must assess them independently. A similar consideration arises when disputes within a family (often over estate matters) result in a splitting of the business assets. One cannot assume that because the two new sets of owners share a family background they, therefore, share the same values. Indeed, the opposite is more often the case.

The third consideration with respect to personal guarantees pertains to the availability of assets. The history of ship finance is full of examples of lenders that lent money because they believed in the assets underlying a personal guarantee. When it became necessary to call the guarantee, they found that the assets either did not exist, could not be found, or were held in the names of family members, trusts, or corporate entities against which the lender had no claim. This even applies to shares in shipowning companies, which given their (usually) bearer nature, legally belong to whoever physically has them in his or her possession at any given point in time.[32] Even when dealing with an owner with a favorable moral track record, a prudent lender looks for comfort only to the owner's other shipping interests, and to other assets only if they are specifically pledged in a well documented, perfected, and enforceable manner. Even with respect to other shipping interests, a lender should be properly skeptical.

If a lender is comfortable with the moral issues involved, he or she must still make a judgment as to whether the personal guarantee has any financial value. Assuming that as noted above, the lender limits his assessment to the owner's other shipowning operations, the analytical approach is quite similar to the approach used in assessing corporate guarantees. However, there are some special problems.

When the shares of the individual shipowning companies are held directly by one or more individuals generally accepted accounting principles do not permit the consolidation of their financial statements. Some shipowners, in an effort to assist (or confuse?) their lenders arrange for their accountants to prepare "combined" financial statements. Analysis of these statements can be useful in much the same way that analysis of consolidated financial statements can be useful, with the caveat that one must be very careful to determine what they actually include. At the simplest level, it is important to ensure that all the shipowning companies, and preferably the management company (ies) (see below) as well are included. Otherwise, results can be distorted, or worse, manipulated.

On another level, combined statements can be prepared on a variety of different bases. Most involve simply adding together the figures for the individual companies. To the extent that transactions between or among the individual companies are not eliminated, such numbers can be very misleading. In particular, liabilities, stockholders' equity, accounts receivable (if any), revenue, and expenses may be double counted. To make these statements useful, one must attempt to ascertain and eliminate the impact of this double counting. Unless the statements have been prepared on a basis that eliminates the intercompany transactions, the identification of these items can be very difficult. Usually, one must depend on the owner's assistance in this respect.

The structure (see Figure 4 for an example) of the typical bulk shipowning group gives rise to another likely distortion. Most groups also include one or more non-shipowning companies that provide various services to all of the shipowning companies. Such services can include (but are not limited to) accounting, chartering, crewing, insurance, other financial services, engineering, and cash management. The legal relationship of this (these) company (ies), which can be loosely classified as management companies, is that of agent[33], not that of parent/subsidiary. They may or may not have common shareholders with the shipowning companies, may or may not also provide services to outside parties, and may have more or less formal contractual relationships with the shipowning companies. The point is that in order to provide these services, a large portion of the group's cash is often held at the management company level. In addition, a variety of expenses related to ship operations is often incurred outside the individual shipowning companies.

Figure 4

Structure of Typical Bulk Shipowning Group

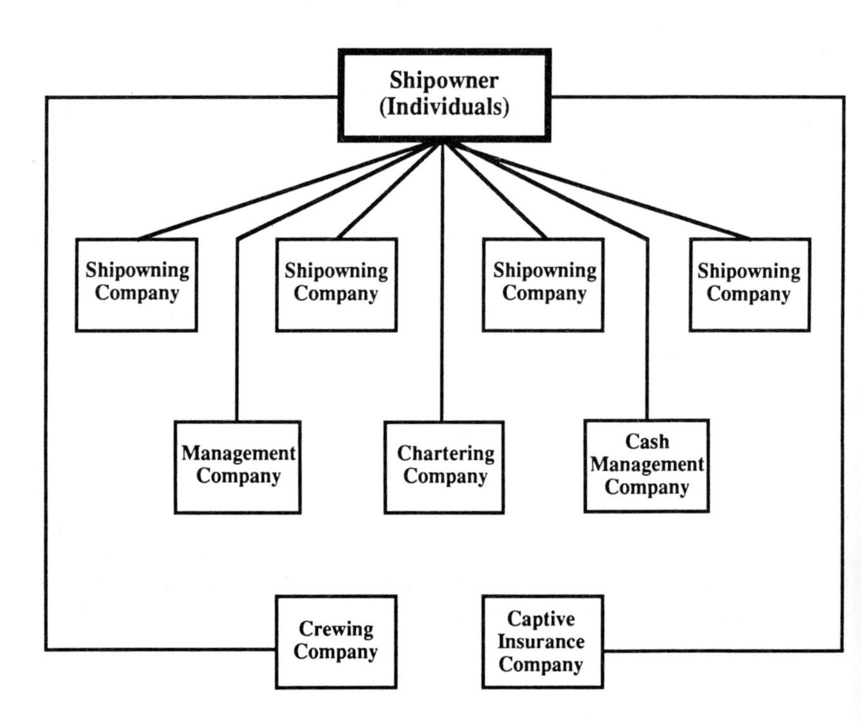

Share Ownership

There are two problems here, one analytical and one practical. From an analytical perspective, failure to include the management companies in the combined financial statements may result in understatement of the shipowning group's overall cash position and expenses. On the other hand, it may lead a lender to be unduly optimistic with respect to the cash that may be available for debt service.

The practical problem is directly related to the latter aspect of the analytical problem. That is, given that the earnings of a financed vessel are normally pledged to the lender, to what extent can the lender take comfort from the management company's holdings of cash that it manages on behalf of the shipowning companies for which it is the managing agent?

If the funds in question are clearly segregated in a separate account this account can be pledged to the lender[34] as additional security. However, the holdings in that account will be the limit of the comfort, as the remainder of the cash in the management company, apart from its own funds, will be the property of other shipowning companies. In addition, if the shipowning group has more than one lender, the other agency accounts may be pledged to other lenders.

Some lenders have attempted to solve this problem by making the management company a party to the loan agreement. This is an imperfect solution for two reasons: first, as noted above, much of the agent's cash will, in fact, be the property of other companies, and hence cannot be used to service the agent's own obligations. Second, there is serious risk that a court will invalidate the management company's obligations as party to the loan agreement if it cannot be demonstrated that the financing results in significant economic benefit to it.

This thorny issue becomes even more difficult if the management company co-mingles the funds of the various shipowning companies for which it provides services. This is a real possibility, particularly if the shipowning companies have common ownership. Similarly, the problem is compounded if cash from the shipowning companies is siphoned off into a separate holding company, as it is difficult to trace the ownership of the funds, and it may be even more difficult to establish economic benefit. Even an honorable shipowner may end up withdrawing funds from a company operating in cash surplus to support a company operating at a cash deficit.

There is only one admittedly imperfect way for a lender to protect itself from this problem. That is to structure the assignment of earnings so that charterhire receipts are paid directly to the lender, with principal and interest payments being withheld before passing any of the funds on to any other company within the group (or external to the group, for that matter). The risk, however, is that the remainder will be insufficient to cover maintenance and operating costs. A company that cannot pay its operating costs cannot perform under its charters and hence cannot earn hire. If the remainder of the group taken as a whole is financially healthy, it may (always assuming that the shipowner is honorable) subsidize the deficit in the operating costs. However, if it is weak, it may be unable to subsidize them, and will most likely approach the lender for an adjustment to the terms of the loan.

This rather lengthy diversion on some of the problems created by the unusual structure of many bulk shipowning groups is intended to warn prospective ship financiers that they should structure their loans with great care, and to be very cautious in attaching meaning to analytical numbers. Shipowning groups should be encouraged to prepare combined financial statements on a sophisticated basis: i.e., with intercompany transactions eliminated and management companies included. Compilation of combined statements from individual statements is tedious in the extreme, particularly if it is the lender that is trying to do the job without the benefit of direct access to the shipowning group's accounting records. It is the kind of work that the owning group's accountants are in a position to do, and the results are worth the effort and cost provided the foregoing limitations are kept in mind.

In the analysis of bulk ship financing transactions, financial statement analysis has its place, though there are distinct limits on its value. For this reason, the discussion so far has not focused on sophisticated analytical techniques. These are rather more relevant to the analysis of liner companies, and will be more fully discussed in that context.

Fleet Cash Flow Analysis

When assessing either corporate or personal guarantees, the analysis of historical financial information is not sufficient. One also has to attempt to forecast the future.

Generally speaking, fleet cash flow analysis is simply the aggregation of the projected cash flow of all the individual ships as discussed earlier in this chapter. However, the fleet with a variety of different types of vessel and vessel employment creates some degree of confusion. How does one project revenues, for example, for a fleet containing a mixture of time charter and spot employment? Even if time charter employment is the dominant factor now, varying terms of the charters may make spot market employment dominant at some time in the future.

The collection and manipulation of the data for a fleet cash flow forecast quickly becomes extremely tedious if the fleet involved is large. The owner is clearly in the best position to do this, and most lenders appreciate being provided with the owner's fleet cash flow forecast,[35] provided that it clearly sets forth the underlying assumptions, and the reasons for choosing those assumptions. However, the lender must independently review the assumptions, with special attention to the issue of spot market freight rates,[36] and the quality of credit risk associated with the time charters. If the fleet can service its debt even when the spot market assumptions are reasonable, one can take considerable comfort in the owner's overall financial strength.

The Multibank Borrower

A small shipowner normally concentrates his business with one lender. Otherwise, there is insufficient ancillary business, such as cash management, current accounts, foreign exchange, and letters of credit to satisfy all the lenders. Likewise, the opportunities for leveraging by cross-collateralization are very restricted.[37]

As an owner grows, however, he should realize that lender capitalization regulations put a legal limit, and portfolio diversification considerations put a prudential limit, on a lender's ability and willingness to support that growth. The owner should give some advance attention to the need for additional sources of financing, as it is unreasonable to expect the rapid response often needed in a sale and purchase transaction from a lender not previously familiar with the owner. An owner with growth plans will find it worth his while to cultivate a select list of potential lenders, providing them with background and fleet information well in advance. It may even be worthwhile to do the first transaction with a new lender on an over-collaterized basis as compensation for the lack of a previous business relationship. If the relationship works, the same assets can usually be leveraged further at a later date. On the other hand, if it does not work, it should not be difficult to subsequently refinance it with yet another lender.

Lenders should be wary of trying to provide all of a growing shipowner's financial requirements. Being a sole lender makes it difficult to be selective: every proposal must be seriously considered, which means that some transactions will be less comfortable than others. Different lenders have different strengths, levels of specialized expertise and experience, and taste for specific types of risk. Thus, having more than one lender adds to flexibility, and tends to increase the comfort level of all lenders.

The multi-lender situation is not, however, without its special risks. Any given lender loses some degree of control, as other lenders may be willing to do things it is not willing to do. The other lenders' policies may have a negative impact beyond the specific transaction involved, as, for instance on the financial strength of the group as a whole, and hence on the value of a corporate or personal guarantee. Furthermore, in the context of a financial restructuring necessitated by an adverse market (and even more so in a workout situation), the multi-lender situation usually results in a struggle for comparative advantage with respect to the assets of the owning group. Much of this could be avoided by the use of inter-creditor agreements, but such agreements are rare in ship finance.

Liner Shipping

The key to a liner company is its ability to provide the level of service appropriate to its given market(s) at any given time. Market share is much more important than with bulk shipping, as it gives the company relatively more control over the pricing in that market, and tends to make it easier to maintain capacity utilization and hence lower the unit price at which the line can break even. This in turn implies an advantage with respect to competition, as the lower the break even, the better the company will be able to perform in an unfavorable market.

To say that the market depends upon supply and demand, though technically true, is not very helpful in understanding the business of a line. Though clearly a line must estimate the future volume and types of cargo movements in its trades, as well as the vessel capacity servicing that trade (or to enter that trade in the future), this is only a starting point. First, it must analyze the pricing structure in that particular market, and how those prices are set. Are prices simply the result of competitive factors, or are they controlled by conferences?[38] Or are they set by the fiat of government regulators? To what extent is the pricing influenced by bilateral agreements between countries in the trading area? These agreements sometimes allocate volumes to specific lines of the respective countries, leaving little or no volume to other parties. This could be either an advantage or a disadvantage depending on the perspective.

Second, a line must consider the level and type of service required and likely to be required in a particular trade, in relation to its own capacity (whether present or to be acquired by charter, second hand purchase, or new construction) and the capacity available from present or potential competition. If shippers require a bi-weekly service, a monthly service may not be able to achieve sufficient market penetration. On the other hand, a bi-weekly service when shippers only require a monthly service may result in insufficient capacity utilization. Again, a container service in a trade dominated by breakbulk goods is likely to suffer from capacity underutilization. On the other hand, if containerization is growing in a particular trade, the first line to provide the necessary capacity may have a competitive advantage. Likewise, other things being equal, the faster a line can move a cargo from origin to destination, the greater its competitive advantage. This involves intermodal considerations.[39] In addition, a vessel that has excess capacity for the trade will suffer from underutilization, while a vessel with insufficient capacity may not be in a position to provide the required level of service. Lastly, given that normally there will never be a perfect fit between the market requirements and the capacity, are there ways to structure the trade so as to gain advantages or offset disadvantages?[40]

Third, a line must consider what kind of sales effort will be required to achieve the desired market penetration; what resources are available to support that effort; and what the cost of that effort will be. Will it use its own cargo solicitation network, contract with an independent agent, or establish its own general agent that in turn will contract with independent sub-agents? Are there competent people available in the local market, and how can they be motivated? A sales strategy will also be required: what type and size of shipper to pursue; to what degree to compete on a price basis in order to achieve or maintain market share; what geographical areas or types of cargo to specialize in; whether and how to advertise; and so on.

The key to the success of the sales/marketing effort will be the nature of the agency network and how it is controlled. Whether it is owned or contracted has a cost implication, as every commission paid to a contracted agent rather than retained by a captive agent reduces the line's overall profitability, though not on a dollar for dollar basis. In considering the agency question, however, the line must also bear in mind the other services its vessels may require, such as bunkers, victuals, port facilities, and stevedoring. These are usually provided or arranged by the sales/marketing agent, and the willingness to provide one service may be related to the rewards of providing other services. Likewise, a contract agent must not be subject to conflicts of interest: mainly, it should not represent two competing lines. Lastly, the agent will hold some of the line' cash (see below), and hence the line wants to feel comfortable with the agent's financial solvency.

Lastly, the line must consider the financial risks involved. Commitment to a trade with specially constructed vessels and containers, an owned agency network, and owned infrastructure (cranes, warehouses, agency offices, etc.) requires a major financial investment, much of which may have to be written off if the returns are found to be unattractive. On the other extreme, a commitment involving chartered vessels, leased containers, a contracted agency network, and contracted or leased infrastructure greatly reduces the financial exposure, but may necessitate compromises that inhibit the performance of the line.

Understanding how a line does its business and what kinds or degrees of risks it assumes is vital to assessing its performance. The analysis of financial statements is rather more useful than in bulk shipping, provided that one is careful to use them as a basis for questions about what lies behind the numbers, rather than simply taking the numbers on faith.

Profit and Loss Statement

Most companies in the liner shipping business are really several lines: that is, they operate lines in more than one trading area. Therefore, their reported financial results reflect the net result of the operation of lines having varied individual results. Examination of certain key numbers and ratios should lead to the right performance questions. These key numbers and ratios are revenues; the ratio of operating income to revenues; the ratio of selling, general and administrative expenses to revenues; the ratio of earnings before interest and taxes to average capitalization;[41] the ratio of the after tax cost of funds[42] to average capitalization; the ratio of income tax to earnings before taxes (the effective tax rate); and the ratio of net profit to average capitalization. Figure 5 is an example of the profit and loss statement for a typical liner company.

When examining revenues (or sales), one runs immediately into a conceptual problem. Most lines account for revenues and vessel expenses on a voyage basis: that is, the basic unit of business results is a single voyage of a single vessel. On the other hand, the result of interest is the performance of the line(s) (which normally involves multiple vessels) over time. A related problem is the accounting for voyages in progress at the close of the accounting period. Some companies recognize revenues and vessel expenses at the beginning of a voyage and consequently the financial statement may include results not yet actually earned. The opposite is true, if, as sometimes happens, a company recognizes revenues and expenses upon completion of a voyage. Although the latter procedure is more conservative, it is equally inaccurate. The distortion tends to grow with the number of vessels in operation. There is a third though seldom used accounting method that prorates the results of an incomplete voyage according to the ratio of the number of voyage days elapsed to the total number of days in the voyage. Since the results of interest are those of a period of time, this method is probably the least misleading.

Perhaps sometime the liner shipping industry will prepare and present its statements on a line basis, but in the meantime there is some comfort in the fact that over time, voyage results should be affected by the same factors that affect line results.

Figure 5

Typical Profit and Loss Statement: Liner Company

(millions: U.S. $)

	12/31/XX	12/31/XY	12/31/XZ
Revenues	384	470	587
Operating Costs	291	336	440
Operating Income	93	134	147
Selling & Admin. Expenses	67	83	127
Earnings Before Interest & Taxes	26	51	20
Interest	14	22	47
Other Income (Expenses)	—	(3)	2
Earnings Before Taxes	12	26	(25)
Income Tax	6	12	—
Net Profit	6	14	(25)
Revenue Increases	17%	22%	25%
Operating Income/Revenues	24%	29%	25%
Selling & Admin. Expenses/Revenues	17%	18%	22%
EBIT***/Average Capitalization*	3%	5%	—
After Tax Cost of Funds**/ Average Capitalization*	3%	3%	8%
Effective Tax Rate	46%	46%	—
Net Profit/Average Capitalization*	2%	3%	—
* Average Capitalization	350	538	640
** Cash Dividends	2	2	3
*** Earnings before Interest and Taxes			

One can easily calculate the direction and rate of growth of sales. Beyond this, the financial statements reveal nothing (although management commentary, which is increasingly required of publicly held companies, may) about the reasons for changes in the sales figures. For example, usually a decline in sales reflects a decline in freight rates, but it may also reflect a decision to reduce capacity, or to withdraw from one or more trades. It is useful to take inflation rates into account here, as a modest nominal decline may hide a rather larger real (after inflation) decline. On the other hand, a real increase in revenues may reflect rising freight rates, increased capacity, or entry into new trades. Furthermore, an increase in overall revenues may hide the fact that revenues rose in some trades and declined in others. It is important to get an explanation for movements in sales figures, if possible on a line basis, because if a liner company has committed resources heavily to a declining trade in such a way as to make it difficult to reduce service without incurring large losses, the resulting losses may well outweigh favorable results in all its other trades put together. Also, sales growth has implications for funding requirements above and beyond the cost of vessel purchases. Unless one is already familiar with most of the company's trades, the only way to get insights into these issues is to have a frank talk with management.

In the case shown in Figure 5, which is based on a now bankrupt U.S. flag liner company,[43] revenues increased by substantial percentages each year. Careful perusal of the company's annual report reveals that the company added large amounts of capacity during these years. In fact, by the third year it had added so much capacity that in an attempt to utilize this capacity adequately, it began to compete aggressively on a price basis. The revenue increases in fact hide a declining trend in the freight rate structure in most of the company's major markets.

The ratio of operating income to revenues is designed to shed some light on the relationship between a liner company's fixed and variable costs.[44] Since a liner company has a relatively high level of fixed assets, one would expect that other things being equal, it would have a relatively high level of fixed costs and, therefore, would be relatively vulnerable to market downturns.

Unfortunately, most financial statements do not provide the kind of volume data necessary for a truly accurate analysis of this problem. However, one can approximate it along the lines suggested in Figure 6, which is simply a manipulation of some of the numbers in Figure 5. As expected, fixed costs are at a high level, which suggests that any given reduction in volume will cause a disproportionate reduction in operating profit. The ratio of operating income to revenues will typically fall if volume is dropping, and this ratio can help to establish whether there is a problem in this respect. It is useful to note that the problem becomes more acute as the proportion of owned

Figure 6

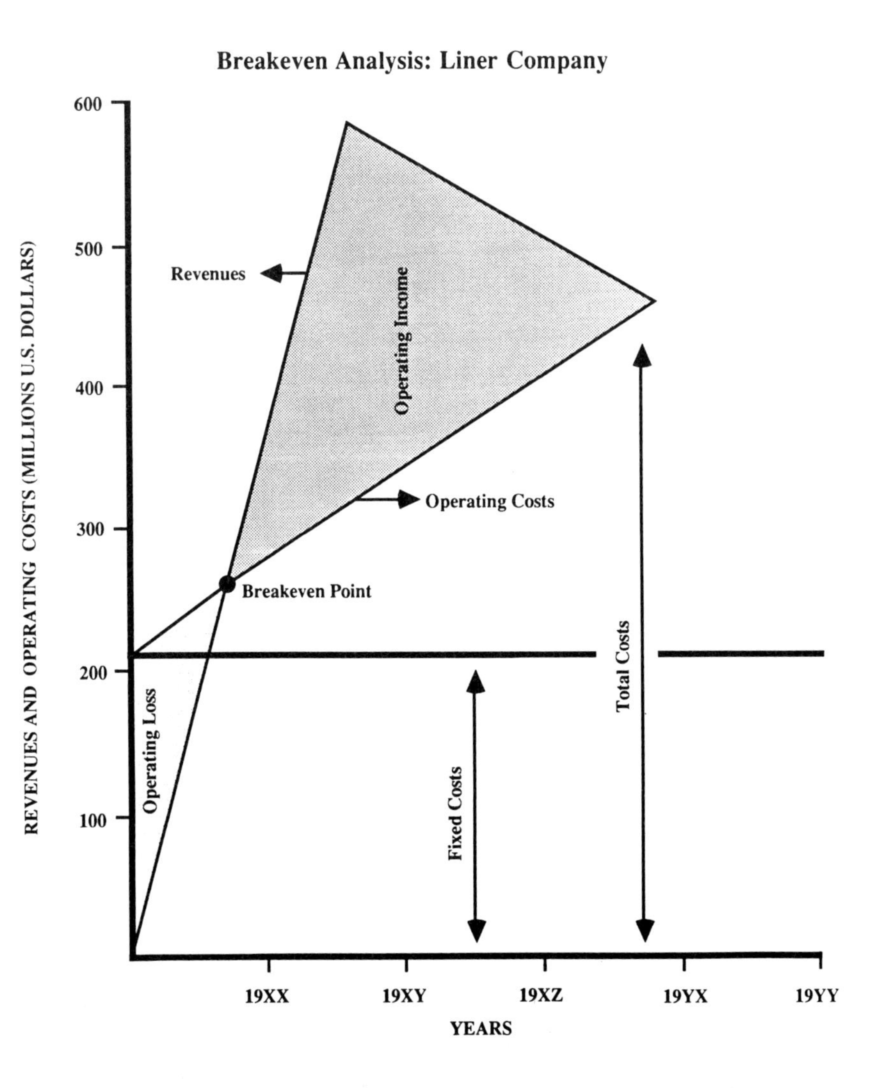
Breakeven Analysis: Liner Company
600
500
400
300
200
100
REVENUES AND OPERATING COSTS (MILLIONS U.S. DOLLARS)
Revenues
Operating Income
Operating Costs
Breakeven Point
Total Costs
Operating Loss
Fixed Costs
19XX
19XY
19XZ
19YX
19YY
YEARS

or chartered (long-term) tonnage increases relative to the proportion of tonnage chartered on a voyage or short-term basis. The shorter the term of the commitment to tonnage, the easier it is to reduce capacity when volume declines. The company in Figures 5 and 6 used no chartered tonnage.

The ratio of selling and administrative expenses is intended to highlight significant changes in this category. Other things being equal, there should be some modest economies of scale as the company grows, unless the company is making major commitments to new trades, in which case the ratio might tend to rise until the company's participation in the trade is established, and then slowly fall off. The company in Figure 5 is an example of the latter scenario, as the new capacity it acquired was employed in new trades.

The ratio of earnings before interest and taxes (EBIT) to average capitalization provides a consistent basis for comparing the overall results of business operations (i.e. excluding the impact of financing decisions) from year to year. Some analysts are tempted to compute a ratio of EBIT to revenues, but as suggested above, trend lines for revenues and expenses rarely if ever move in parallel and, therefore, such a calculation is not terribly meaningful. Likewise, some analysts compute a negative ratio if the company is in a loss position. This is a mistake born of habit, as a negative margin makes no conceptual sense.

The remaining three ratios aim at understanding the impact of financing decisions. The underlying idea is that unless a company can earn a return on its capital employed in excess of the cash cost of that capital, its capital investment decisions will not be self-sustaining. Its only recourse will be to reduce that cash cost, and to the extent that its capital consists of borrowed money and (to a lesser degree) preferred stock rather than common equity, its flexibility to do so will be limited.

One can determine whether this is an issue to be concerned about by comparing the after tax cost of funds to the return on average capitalization. If the former is equal to or greater than the latter, there is a serious problem worthy of further analysis. In the case of the company in Figure 5, the after tax cost of funds equalled or exceeded the return on capitalization for three consecutive years, and thus the basis of its financial difficulties was apparent well in advance. It is also worth noting that for a company that is subject to income tax, the after tax cost of debt rises sharply as the company moves into a loss position, i.e., precisely when it is least convenient. This happens because the tax deductibility of interest is a benefit only as long as there are sufficient earnings from operations to fully offset the interest expense. In other words, the company must now generate more cash to meet the same level of interest payments, because now, no portion of the interest payments can be offset against income taxes.

Statement of Changes in Financial Position

In general, sources and uses of funds analysis is done in the same way and for the same purpose as it is done for bulk shipping companies. The only significant differences are in the realm of net working investment and short-term borrowings.

As noted earlier, bulk shipping companies rarely have any need for accounts receivable and inventory, but do benefit from credit terms for bunkers and, to a lesser degree, wage accruals. Thus, their net working investment requirements are negative and, therefore, a source of funds.

While liner companies also have little or nothing in the way of requirements to maintain inventories, they usually do have a requirement to extend credit. If a liner company is a member of conferences, the conferences usually determine the terms on which credit may be extended in the relevant trade. In many conferences, credit terms are theoretically subject to audit and sanctions by the conference, though it is questionable how effective this is. In any case, the resulting accounts receivable give rise to a funding requirement. Like a bulk shipping company, a liner company can usually buy bunkers on credit terms, and whether this credit is sufficient to fully fund the receivables depends on the relationship between the turnover of accounts receivable and the turnover of accounts payable.

The turnover of accounts receivable is often described in terms of an average collection period: i.e., the average number of days required to collect an account.[45] This period depends not only on the credit terms on which business is done, but also on the "quality" of the receivables (i.e., shippers' willingness and ability to pay within credit terms) and the terms of agency contracts (if agency functions have been contracted to one or more third parties). Most such agency contracts call for the agent to collect all accounts receivable due in the geographical area it is responsible for, and remit them on to the line on a predetermined schedule more closely associated with satisfaction of the obligations incurred by the line at the related port of call than with the actual timing of the collection. In other words, the agents also incur obligations on behalf of the line, and tend to hold back remittance of collections not only until the receivables are collected, but also until all billings for obligations incurred have been received and paid. Thus, the line's actual receipt of the funds is likely to be delayed beyond the credit terms extended. In recent years, in an effort to improve lines' cash management, there has been some tendency to rewrite agency contracts on a basis calling for weekly or bi-weekly remittance of collections, with separate advance funding of obligations incurred. This has resulted in a very limited improvement in the average collection period, although admittedly at the expense of advance funding.

The principal source of funds underlying a line's net working investment is credit for bunker purchases, and the amount of that source depends on the volume of bunker purchases and the terms available, usually 60-90 days. It is possible that at any given time, this source will not be sufficient to fully fund the requirement to extend credit. Thus, there may be a net funding requirement.

In the liner shipping industry, this funding requirement is usually met either by drawing upon the liquidity reserve, or by borrowing on a short-term basis. If lenders perceive a company to be financially strong, the company may be able to borrow on an unsecured basis. It is more common, however, for such financings to be secured by some form of lien on or pledge of accounts receivable. Lenders will usually advance up to 80% of the face amount of invoices or manifests they consider "eligible," that is, of acceptable credit quality in their sole judgment. Whether lending on a secured or unsecured basis, lenders will expect to be repaid from the collection of the related receivables.[46]

For a lender asked to accommodate a line with this sort of short-term borrowing facility, the critical issue is the quality of the receivables. Although comparison of the average collection period with the normal credit terms extended, and analysis of the movements in the company's reserve for bad debts will shed some light on this problem, a lender should usually request a list of major shippers, and an ageing of the receivables. An ageing is simply a list indicating the status of receivable collections relative to their terms: i.e., thirty days overdue, sixty days overdue, etc. This information provides a basis for checking on the credit standing of the individual accounts. If the lender intends to extend credit on a secured basis, it should also ensure as much as possible that the accounts are not subject to a prior lien.[47]

In all other respects, sources and uses of funds analysis for a liner company can proceed exactly as for a bulk shipping company. A liner company will have additional fixed asset requirements, such as containers, chassis, loading/unloading equipment, and the appurtenances of intermodalism to the extent that these are owned rather than leased. They may be independently financed. The analytical techniques, though, are no different.

Balance Sheet

Under most scenarios, a liner company's short-term liquidity is not a major problem. Usually, short-term borrowings can be arranged to cover any shortfall in net working investment requirements. When liquidity problems arise, it is almost always because of the company's heavy commitment to capital (fixed) assets, and decisions as to how to finance those assets.

The critical question then becomes how much debt is too much, and unfortunately, traditional debt/equity ratios are not very helpful in this regard. As a lender, there is some point to calculating a fleet finance ratio, but the purpose of doing this is to assess the risk of becoming undersecured[48] rather than to determine what level of debt could become a threat to ongoing operations.

There are a number of ratios that financial analysts habitually calculate in an attempt to get a handle on this problem. These include, but are not limited to, ratio of EBIT to interest; a fixed charge ratio;[49] and a cash flow to total debt ratio, each of which has some limited usefulness. However, these ratios take into account neither the structure of the debt nor the cyclicality of earnings.

In order to assess the company's ability to service its obligations, one must attempt to forecast future results (see below). Then one must judge what portion of the cash flow can be counted upon even at the bottom of a cycle, bearing in mind that a liner company, to the extent that it owns its tonnage and generates large amounts of non-cash expense, may generate quite a lot of cash from its operations even when it is not profitable. That stable portion of the cash flow plus that portion of the liquidity reserve not required for day to day business operations, can suggest the amount of debt and the repayment schedule that a company can safely tolerate in a worst-case scenario. The limited factor is the maximum repayment term that lenders will allow. Unless it is willing to assume that surplus cash flow from good years will be available to offset a shortfall in bad years, it will be difficult for a lender to feel comfortable with much debt beyond this level, as higher levels will make a restructuring (or worse) almost inevitable. Likewise, if the amount of debt is acceptable but the maturity schedule calls for repayments in excess of what the annual "stable" cash flow can service, a restructuring of the debt may be in order. This can be an opportunity for a perceptive lender.

Projections

It should be clear by now that it is impossible to assess a liner ship financing without attempting to project future results. It is much more difficult to be sophisticated about this than is the case with a bulk shipping company.

Although analysis on a service basis would be a better guide to profitability, most cash flow forecasts for liner companies are based on typical voyages, much as described earlier on in the section on forecasting for contract of affreightment bulk shipping transactions. However, it is necessary to make many more assumptions, particularly as to freight rates (determined by conferences if the line is a conference operator, but given some stability to the extent that there are underlying contracts of affreightment); capacity utilization (otherwise known as the load factor); operating costs; voyage costs (bunker consumption and prices, port costs, stevedoring, agency, etc.); marketing costs; the investment in peripheral infrastructure, such as containers, chassis, loading and unloading equipment, terminals and warehouses, and intermodal equipment, that will enable the company to meet its marketing objectives; and taxation. This will result in a net figure that can be adjusted to reflect the specific transaction under consideration.

With respect to existing obligations, the information should be readily available in the financial statements, or at least obtainable from management. However, one must be careful to ensure that all relevant obligations are included. That certain categories of debt, such as bank term loans and official export credits, should be included goes without saying. Less obvious is that subordinated debt and redeemable preferred stock should also be included. The less preferred position of these obligations with respect to the assets of the company is usually relevant only in a bankruptcy or liquidation situation, as they have ongoing servicing requirements.[50] More subtle yet are certain contingent liabilities, such as guarantees of obligations of unconsolidated affiliated companies; unfunded investment commitments (such as, for instance, orders for vessels to be constructed); and liabilities for unfunded social benefits. One should bear in mind that what is of interest is not just the total of the obligations outstanding, but the servicing requirements for a relevant number of years in the future (for the term of the credit facility envisaged, for instance). The debt service figures so obtained can then be adjusted to reflect the transaction in question, thus completing the cash flow statement.

The forecasting procedure described above sounds simple, and mechanically speaking, is indeed simple. In fact, the easiest and most effective analytical approach is to use a computerized spread sheet program to design a simple model. The difficulty is in deriving the appropriate assumptions, which are not all apt to be readily available to a lender.

The prospective borrower is apt to be in a better position to provide useful assumptions, and the best procedure is to start with its projections, with clearly stated assumptions. However, it is imperative to test those assumptions.[51] The first step is to put them into the spread sheet model, and experiment with changes. By seeing the impact of these changes on the results, one can quickly determine the most critical variables, and proceed to check those against external evidence.

Freight rates are always a critical variable, and these can be checked for reasonableness against published sources such as (in the U.S.) the *Journal of Commerce,* freight rates quoted by other lines in the same trade, and/or conference rate schedules, which are routinely published. In addition to checking the rates themselves, one must also assess the assumed rate of growth. This is directly linked to the future demand/capacity relationship in the trade, and though a more judgemental issue, close following of the industry press[52] will usually reveal obvious inconsistencies. For example, one would be justifiably suspicious of an assumption of 10% per annum growth, if one was aware that capacity was about to be added to an already overtonnaged trade. The volume issue is similarly judgemental, and if the transaction involves entry into a new trade, the line should be prepared to provide a copy of its feasibility study.

Operating costs can be checked against historical results, and if there is a significant discrepancy, the line should be prepared to explain. Bunker prices are routinely published in the industry press, and consumption rates should be included with the vessel specifications. Other voyage costs tend not to be critical variables, but if they are, they can be cross checked with agents familiar with the trade. The same is true for marketing costs and the investment in peripheral infrastructure.

Once one has tested the assumptions for criticality and reasonableness, one can return to the model and change those assumptions that seem overly optimistic. If the results remain favorable, "what if" analysis is in order in an effort to determine what the level of "stable" cash flow is. One can also experiment with the structure in an effort to determine whether there is a better way to do the transactions.[53]

Security

Most vessel financings for liner companies are done on a secured basis. The security package is much the same as for a bulk shipping company, but with two differences. Both differences reflect the peculiar nature of a line's business. In bulk shipping groups, each vessel is typically owned by a separate corporate entity. However, because the fundamental business of a line is the operation of a service rather than vessel ownership and operation, the ownership of multiple vessels in a single corporate entity is much more common. This is particularly true of national flag lines, although when a line owns vessels flying a flag other than that of its home country, the one ship/one company structure once again becomes the norm.[54] In this case, usually the foreign flag vessels are time chartered to the line.

One of the problems with both liner company structures is that there is no feasible way to structure an assignment of earnings that has any value. The earnings stream that underlies any given transaction is the earnings stream of the line, not of any individual vessel. When the vessels are owned by special purpose companies, and time chartered to the line, the value of the assignment may be more illusory than real. This is because the ability of the line to pay the charterhire will depend on the line's success in operating its various services.

The other difference pertains to corporate guarantees. In the case of the multi-ship owning company, a corporate guarantee is, of course, conceptual nonsense. However, in the case of the other structure, the line's corporate guarantee is usually appropriate given that the ultimate source of repayment is the earnings of the line. If the transaction is to be done solely on the basis of a time charter to the line, one must still assess the commercial viability of the line; one must pay special attention to the terms of the charter; and the financial rewards should be appropriately greater.[55]

Vessel Operating Pools

A vessel operating pool is an association of vessels, the physical operations of which are managed or arranged for by their owners, that contracts with a third party (usually one of the owners) for the marketing of all the vessels. The pool manager receives a fee for its services, and the pool profits are shared by the members on some sort of pari-passu basis. The theory is that superior market intelligence and performance standards and greater employment flexibility will allow the pooled vessels to earn a premium over what they could earn if employed separately in the open market. The arrangement is particularly common in Scandinavia, and has been known to pertain to various types of bulk ships. For instance, it heavily dominates the parcel tanker business, but pools of dry bulkcarriers, tankers, and combination carriers have also operated effectively.

The analysis of a transaction involving a vessel to be employed in a pool is little different from the analysis for a vessel to be employed under a contract of affreightment, or in the spot market. However, it is important to examine the historical average rate performance of the pool to see if it has in fact achieved premium rates. Only then can premium rates be incorporated in a cash flow forecast. It is also important to examine the vessel's contract with the pool and the pool manager in order to be clear about the costs of membership, audit rights, and the timing of earnings flows. The timing of earnings flows is particularly important, as these flows should largely determine the repayment schedule for the loan.

The assignment of earnings that pertains to a vessel employed in an operating pool will have a slightly different character than the one normal in bulk shipping. That is, the earnings assigned will be the payments from the pool to the owner that relate to the specific vessel, rather than hire or contract payments from ultimate employers. Provided the pool arrangement is a clean one (and one can independently verify the reputation of the pool manager), this different character should not be a problem.

Country Risk

Lenders often have major difficulties in assigning country risk to ship financing transactions. The country risk of ship financings, particularly in the bulk sector, is often very difficult to determine. For instance, one small tanker fleet is owned by a family of Chinese extraction, flies the Liberian flag, trades worldwide, has mostly U.S. and European charterers, and is managed from two offices, one in the U.S. and one in the U.K. This is not at all unusual.

Furthermore, the use of flags of convenience creates a severe distortion. When the Liberian registry is managed by a U.S. company; Liberian flag vessels rarely even approach Liberia; and (because they maintain their bank accounts usually in New York, London, or Geneva) are not subject to present or future Liberian foreign exchange controls, it is clear that Liberia has little or nothing to do with the risk.

In addition, the secured nature of most ship financings, puts them in a special category: if a country has financial difficulties the lender still has recourse to a tangible asset that can be sold internationally. The risk then becomes a risk on the rules of the flag as described earlier in this chapter.

This is not to say that there are no obvious elements of country risk in ship financings. Where a general cargo or container line is involved, much depends on the status of trade between the two countries. In bulk shipping the country risk of the charterer can be an important factor. The difficulties of the Eddie Steamship Group originated with its grain contract with the Philippine National Lines. Freights were payable upon loading, but because for a time the charterer was unable to issue letters of credit, there were no loadings. Vessels sat idle, incurring expenses but earning no income. Eventually the owner ran out of cash.

Generally speaking, ship financings are not included in general country debt reschedulings, except when the borrower is a state-owned entity, or when the loan is covered by a bank guarantee as sometimes happens with shipowners from developing countries, with shipowners with little or no operating track record, or when the vessel will fly a flag with a mortgage law unacceptable to lenders.

The relationship between country risk and ship finance is an ambiguous one, which even bank regulators and auditors have failed to resolve. Lender portfolio analysts would do well to establish a new category of "shipping risks", to include all those ship financings in which the primary risk is on the shipping markets rather than on a country.

Many ship finance specialists, taking comfort from the secured nature of the transactions and the priority with respect to foreign exchange often enjoyed by shipowners, take country risks rather lightly. To a large degree, the comforting factors are real. However, there are a few important issues that should be born in mind.

First, the primary country risks for a shipowner are political rather than economic. Some of these were described earlier in this chapter, but others have a somewhat different slant. For example, the status of the relations between a flag country and a chartering country can pose a serious risk to the success of the transaction. Flying a flag of convenience is not necessarily any protection. There is a reason why U.S. based Liberian flag shipowners should not employ their ships with Cuban charterers,[56] but this is a question of law. More subtle is the question of future relations with countries, trading with which is not a matter of law. A U.S. based shipowner with a vessel chartered to the National Iranian Oil Company when Iran was governed by the Shah would be in a fairly comfortable position, but the same charter might be rather vulnerable under the succeeding government. A shipowner who could foresee the forthcoming changes would be in a position to take protective action.

As another example, the internal political dynamics of a flag or chartering country may pose a problem. A charter to a state owned oil company may be invalidated if, as the result of a change of government, it becomes apparent that the terms of the charter were not commercially justifiable.

Finally, geopolitics may play a role. One of the major factors in tanker trading in recent years has been the deliberate effort of the United States to diversify its sources of supply of crude oil away from the Middle East. The increasing importance of Mexican crude was not merely a question of convenience, but was also the result of a deliberate policy that had a political purpose. This policy has had a major impact on the supply and demand for certain sizes of tankers, as very large crude carriers were not appropriate for the Mexican trade.

Second, the economic aspect of country risk is far from totally absent, especially for liner companies that do not have much flexibility to change their services to meet changes in trading patterns. A liner company depending heavily on trade with one country, that would also normally trade to countries in between, will have to continue trading to that country despite a drop off in trade involving the intervening countries. The line will not have the flexibility (as a bulk ship might) to reemploy the vessel in a completely different market. Again, a country with a foreign exchange problem may aggressively pursue exports while restricting imports. The inability to find a cargo to this country will be a powerful disincentive to the owner of a ship to put it in position to carry the exports.

In addition, the foreign exchange problem never totally disappears. It is true that charterers importing cargoes perceived as essential will usually be allowed to pay charterhire, even when a country has a severe foreign exchange problem. For example, throughout Brazil's foreign exchange problems of recent years, Petrobas (the Brazilian state oil company) has continued to pay its charterhire obligations. In a similar vein, domestic flag shipowners, whether government or privately owned, are usually viewed by their governments as foreign exchange earners (or at least conservers: domestic tonnage used represents a reduction in charterhire that must be paid abroad), and consequently are usually given priority access to the foreign exchange needed to meet vessel obligations incurred abroad.

However, the definition of an essential cargo is necessarily rather vague. One of the risks faced by a bulk shipowner is that a cargo once described in law as essential is reclassified. With foreign exchange no longer available, a shipper may no longer be able to meet its obligations under a time charter. Likewise, if a country has a foreign exchange problem and consequently restricts its imports, the balance of currencies earned by a liner based there will shift unfavorably. If the liner has difficulty convincing the relevant authorities of this fact, it may find itself unable to pay its foreign currency obligations.[57]

There is a concept in lending known as sovereign risk; that is, a borrowing entity is construed to be the same risk as the government of that country. If the transaction is government guaranteed, or if the government is by law responsible for the obligations of a commercial entity, the case for considering it as sovereign risk is very strong. The case is also very strong for obligations of a government agency, but the political implications may be rather unsavory. For example, the Brazilian government has treated SUNAMAM's (the merchant marine regulatory agency) foreign obligations as its own. However, investigations into its operations revealed activities that responsible officials disclaimed responsibility for. Even inadvertent involvement in such marginal activities could be very embarrassing to a foreign lender.

The case for sovereign risk becomes much weaker at other levels. Some have argued that sovereign risk considerations should also apply to commercial ventures whose shares are government owned; ventures with some shares in government hands, and some in private hands; and even to some totally private ventures in "critical" lines of business.[58] The argument always goes that the economic sector involved is so politically or economically important that the government cannot allow it to fail. In a few cases (more and more in recent years) there is even a track record of government support, but usually there is little credible evidence to support these assertions. The number of cases in which governments have refused to support these borderline cases has also grown rapidly in recent years, and therefore it is dangerous to assume that a borrowing or chartering entity is a sovereign risk unless its obligations are explicitly, in one way or another the obligations of the government. This even applies to banks issuing loan guarantees: the presumption that a failing bank will receive government support has increasingly in recent years been found to be invalid. With the possible exception of central banks, the financial strength of banks must be assessed on their own merits.

At this stage, one might well ask what benefit there is to being considered a sovereign risk? Clearly the financial strength of a sovereign risk can be no greater than that of the government in question. By the same token, a government whose financial strength is declining, will be less likely to support "quasi" sovereign entities than a government in a strong financial position. If the government in question is truly weak, the greatest virtue is that the obligations of the sovereign risk entity will be included in any general rescheduling of the government's obligations.

Given this unexciting prospect, lenders and shipowners might do well to do business only with entities regardless of ownership, that are commercially viable; provide a service (or trade in commodity) perceived as essential; and earn from their own operations sufficient foreign exchange, which they are able to keep under their own control,[59] to cover their obligations. Even commercially available country risk insurance is of little help. Generally speaking, insurance underwriters will not cover those risks for which one truly needs the cover.

Notes

1. It is important to distinguish consolidated statements from so-called combined statements. The latter merely add up the financial figures for all the companies in the group, whereas the former eliminate the intercompany transactions.

2. There is good reason to suspect that had the lenders to Hellenic Lines required and reviewed audited financial statements rather than the unaudited figures provided by the company, their losses from Hellenic's eventual bankruptcy would have been significantly less than they actually were.

3. For those lenders not yet conversant with shipping, every vessel, when constructed, is certified by any one of a number of national organizations (the classification societies) to have met a specified set of standards (i.e. that it is "in class"). Thereafter, all surveys, major overhauls, significant changes, etc. are recorded in the vessel's records and certified by the classification society. Thus, a set of classification society records, provided they are certified by a reputable society, should provide useful clues to the condition of the vessel.

4. On a strictly theoretical basis, the value of a vessel should be the present value of all future cash flows from operating it. Clearly, this involves various subjective assumptions as to expected future freight rates, inflation rates, required return on capital, etc. The most critical of these is expected future freight rates, and since views on this subject change constantly, it should come as no surprise that values constantly change.

5. A security maintenance clause is a requirement in a loan agreement that the borrower never allow the finance ratio to exceed a specified level. If that level is exceeded, the borrower must either prepay a portion of the loan, or provide additional collateral. The working viability of such a clause depends on the availability of sufficient cash or additional collateral, but at the very least, such a clause gives the lender the right to foreclose before the value of the vessel shrinks below the amount of the loan. In any case, the valuation issue can be rather sticky here. It can also be an issue if there is more than one vessel in the collateral package, and a vessel is sold. How it is resolved depends largely on the relative strengths of the borrower's and lender's negotiating position, but a common compromise, if values are in dispute, is to go by the arithmetic mean of the various valuations received.

6. Imagine a ULCC's trying to find a cargo of crude oil to carry to the Arabian Gulf, for instance. The development of the combination carrier concept was an attempt to solve this problem, and make it possible for a vessel trading one direction with oil to return with grain, ore, or some other dry cargo. The results have been mixed:

some owners have managed to cross trade successfully. All too often, however, combination carriers have tended to trade exclusively in either liquid or dry cargo (depending on the relative strengths of the two markets), and hence have not justified the premium of up to 25% in their construction cost.

7. An earnings recapture clause is a provision incorporated in some loan agreements that requires the shipowner to apply an agreed portion of the vessel's surplus cash flow (as defined in the loan agreement) to prepay installments due in the inverse order of their maturity. It is worth noting that this kind of provision wreaks havoc with fixed rate loans because of the lender's inability to predetermine the amount and term of the required funding. There are two possible solutions to the dilemma. First, instead of applying the prepayment amounts to the debt, they can be placed on deposit and pledged as additional collateral, which accomplishes the same purpose. Second, the loan can be broken into two parts, one on a fixed rate basis, and one on a floating rate basis, with the prepayments applied to the latter part.

8. Many of the lenders to the W.H. Eddie Hsu Group (Eddie Steamship, et al) of Taipei managed to convince themselves that because of its close relationship with the Republic of China government, the Hsu Group was insulated from unfavorable changes in its COA rates from China Steel and Taiwan Power. The fact that this was not in fact true was major contributor to the financial difficulties of the Hsu Group, and resulted in heavy losses to the lenders.

9. Given many lenders' involvement in the foreign exchange and interest rate futures markets, this concept may be easier for them to absorb than for shipowners. The idea is to buy or sell contracts forward so as to ensure a level of profitability: unsatisfactory results from vessel operations can be offset by profits from contract trading, and vice versa. Unlike most commodities futures contracts, freight futures contracts are defined in terms of an index, with all settlements in cash. Freight rate futures contracts are actively traded on the London based Baltic International Freight Futures Exchange (BIFFEX), and on the Bermuda based INTEX. These exchanges use the same index.

Further discussion of this concept would be quite technical. Additional general information can be found in Barry Parker's two excellent articles entitled ''Fuelling Futures'' in the April and May/June, 1986 issues of *Seatrade Business Review* or from any freight rate futures broker such as E.D. & F. Man.

10. Unfortunately, very few lenders do an adequate job of what-if analysis. There are two principal reasons for this. First, the analytical work on ship financing transactions tends to be done by the ship financing unit of the lender, rather than in a separate, independent credit department as would be normal for most other financing proposals. As a result, the cash flow figures tend to be used more as a tool for selling the transaction to credit committees than for risk assessment. This is too bad, as it leads lending officers to have too much faith in the validity of assumptions that credit committees are not in a position to second guess. Second, lending officers frequently fear that what-if analyses showing unfavorable results will come back to haunt them later if the transaction does not turn out as expected. Absent abuse of the what-if concept, this should not be a problem, but as a practical matter is probably a valid concern. Perhaps this is another argument for analysis by an independent unit. Independent analysis would force loan officers to justify in advance why certain what-if results should be ignored or at least viewed as acceptable risks.

11. This is largely because banks as a group find counter cyclical thinking very difficult, even when it has a favorable impact on their assets' risk profile.

12. As used here and hereafter, the term "time charter equivalent" refers to the spot freight less the related voyage costs.

13. I am reminded of an Ernest Hemingway novel in which one character, when asked how he went bankrupt, replied: "At first very slowly, and then all of a sudden."

14. Mr. Paul Slater has scoffed at this notion, and expressed the thought that this means the owner is dealing with the wrong charterers. To the extent that a moral question is involved, I agree. However, I perceive an economic issue as well. That is, if a charterer is a company, such as another shipowner, for which freight is a major component of its costs, it may well be unrealistic to continue the higher time charter rate, as the result may be the complete disappearance of that business. Clearly there can be a preference for business with charterers, such as major oil companies, for which freight is a relatively unimportant component of the cost structure. However, to categorically rule out the other business would be to unduly restrict the potential market.

15. Well established shipowners sometimes use third party (i.e. unaffiliated) vessel managers in order to take advantage of lower costs that may be available in other jurisdictions. In other cases, where a prospective shipowner has no operating track record, use of a third party manager that has a track record can insulate lenders from operating competence risk until the new owner's learning curve reaches an acceptable level.

16. In this respect, a current court case is most instructive. Prudential Line was forced into bankruptcy by its creditors in September, 1986. Three vessels had previously been arrested, by a bank in May, 1986, and the U.S. Maritime Administration (MARAD), a U.S. government agency which had guaranteed the financing, paid over $12 million to the bank the following month, simultaneously entering into possession of the vessels, which were in lay-up. Prudential brought legal action seeking to enjoin the sale of the vessels until court approval was obtained, whereas Marad argued that under a recently passed law intended to expedite its ability to foreclose on defaulted loans, it was entitled to sell the vessels ninety days after the bankruptcy filing. The U.S. bankruptcy court judge enjoined the sale pending a decision on this issue, although in partial compensation for lay-up costs, he required Prudential to post a bond of $125,000 for each month until the issue was settled. Thus, many months after the vessels' arrest, a U.S. government mortgage holder had still been unable to realize any value from its collateral, and there was no end in sight.

17. In this respect the U.S. Lines bankruptcy case should be interesting. The Export-Import Bank of Korea, presumably through a U.S. bank trustee, holds second mortgages over the twelve large containerships.

18. With the sharp drop in oil prices in the last few years, this kind of subsidy is clearly less valuable than it used to be.

19. This is a reference to the borrower's political and social connections. However, in this realm, one must be especially cautious, as the borrower's claims cannot always be taken at face value. I am put in mind of a certain Saudi Arabian businessman who claimed to have close connections to the Saudi royal family. These claims were picked up by the western press, which did not realize that the Saudi royal family is very large (and hence that such connections were not necessarily of any particular value), and that other Saudi businessmen regarded the individual in question as thoroughly disreputable. Again, connections may be real, but be of an unsavory nature, as when charters at rates significantly above the market are arranged by feeding the Swiss bank accounts of government officials, or granting connected people economic interests in a project on particularly favorable terms. Unexpected publicity can cause such projects to come unwound very quickly. Further, political prominence may be more apparent than real. I am aware of a Greek shipowner who rose to a prominent position in the Greek Shipowners' Association not because of any perceived connections or even leadership qualities, but simply because no one else wanted the job. Lastly, connections may be attributable to political affiliations, and if the government group or party changes, such connections may be of transitory value. Lenders are particularly vulnerable: not only can they lose the benefit of the owner's alleged connections, but they become tarred with their client's brush, and may consequently find it difficult to do business with other borrowers in that country.

20. Including one shipowning company that is a subsidiary of a major corporation controlled by the Brazilian state.

21. As an officer doing Greek flag ship financing from the Cayman Islands branch of a Dutch bank, I used financing documents governed by the laws of the State of New York. The same bank, doing Greek flag ship financing through its branch in Piraeus, Greece, used documents governed by Greek law.

22. The lender is entitled to rely upon this. I am aware of a situation in which a broker's acknowledgement received by the lender at the closing of a financing was held to be binding on the underwriters, despite non-payment of premiums, when the vessel became a total loss three months later. In fact, the underwriters made no attempt to challenge it, although they did withhold the premiums due from the claim payment. Despite this, I believe that requiring evidence of premium payments may save a great deal of heartache in the event of such admittedly unusual circumstances.

23. The practice of requiring insurance in excess of the loan amount is designed to provide for accrued but unpaid interest, and amounts that the lender may have advanced under the mortgage for insurance premiums, maintenance, or other disbursements the owner may have, for one reason or another not been in a position to pay. This practice of maintaining excess cover has not been particularly controversial. What has become somewhat controversial, is the practice of relating insurance amounts to loan values at all. Underwriters have become aware, particularly as ship values have shrunk drastically in the last few years, that they have in certain limited circumstances been in effect ensuring repayment of loans. There are two primary concerns here. First, as the spread between the insured value and the market value widens, it is increasingly tempting for an owner to deliberately arrange for the vessel to become a total loss. It is very difficult to prove malfeasance or gross negligence in these cases, as a result of which the underwriters are likely to be required to pay the claim anyway. By the same token, the shrinking market values reduce anything that the underwriters might be able to recover from the hull. The solution to this dilemma is far from clear, although it is almost certain to exert upward pressure on premiums. As a side note on the malfeasance issue, the underwriters typically impose a far greater burden of proof on the owner if the vessel is over fifteen years old, which is perhaps another reason, from the perspectives of both lender and owner, to be involved only in relatively modern tonnage. I am aware of a situation in which the under-writers fell victim to their own complaint. On a vessel over twenty years old, and worth less than $500,000, they refused to consider providing less than $1,500,000 of cover, even though $250,000 would have satisfied the bank. When the vessel became a total loss, attempts to prove malfeasance utterly failed, and they were forced to pay out the full face amount of the policy.

24. A few banks, such as Citibank and Bankers Trust, that have made a specialty of providing services to the insurance industry, may be exceptions to this rule.

25. I am not aware of a single case in which mortgagee's interest insurance prevented or reduced a loss from a ship financing transaction.

26. Not to be confused with "cut through language," which may not be enforceable.

27. Guarantee, as used here, means a legal obligation on the part of one party for specified obligations of another party. It does not mean, as it apparently is construed to mean in some countries, the pledging of other assets unless such pledging is specifically provided for in separate legal documents.

28. I have more than once found owners suddenly finding their cash running out, without having a clear idea why. A look at the aggregate sources and uses of funds over the previous few years was very revealing.

29. For this concept I am indebted to Mr. Carl Samuelson, a long time credit officer at the Morgan Guaranty Trust Company, now in business as a consultant on risk analysis and decision making in financial institutions.

30. The one year term applies in the United States, the United Kingdom, and many other countries, but is not universally applicable. I have seen current asset and current liability terms ranging from six months to four years, and in these situations, the meaning of net working capital is clearly quite different.

31. If, for some reason, credit terms such as these are not available (usually because of the owner's lack of a credit history with the major oil companies), the banker can provide a useful service by issuing standby letters of credit to cover bunker payments, and hencc, by substituting the risk of the bank for the risk of the owner, opening up this inexpensive source of credit.

32. I have even heard of a case in which the legal owner of shares in a ship-owning company was a dog owned by the personal guarantor. These shares were not available to creditors.

33. This legal concept is very common in the shipping industry. It simply refers to a party (usually corporate) that is empowered by contract to act on behalf of another in more or less limited ways as defined in the contract, without becoming responsible for the liabilities of the party on behalf of which it is acting.

34. There is precedent for this, as courts have generally upheld the concept that such funds in segregated agency accounts are the property of the shipowning company, not the agent. However, it is important to properly document the pledge. In addition to normal account documentation, which is usually provided and signed by the agent, it is necessary to ensure that there is clear evidence of the agent's authority to pledge the account.

35. As a practical matter, lenders should not expect to receive fleet cash flow forecasts from small shipowners. However, if the owner provides a proper information package (see Appendix B), preparation of such a forecast will not be unduly cumbersome.

36. Assuming the availability of a personal computer and a suitable spreadsheet program, some "what if" analysis may be appropriate.

37. If a lender perceives the finance ratio of its collateral as low, it may be willing to advance additional funds by cross collateralizing the new borrowings with previously existing collateral. However, if the owner's business is spread too thinly, other lenders will have prior claims on the assets, and consequently the lender may be unwilling to make the additional advances.

38. Conferences are simply legal price fixing cartels for specific trading areas, and are usually major factors in the pricing in any given market. However, their influence is not unlimited. First, membership is not compulsory, and hence there is always the threat, real or implied, of competition from non-members. There are many cases of member lines becoming non-member lines when they felt the pricing structure was costing them market share. Second, increasingly lines and conferences are being forced by competitive factors and/or by law to negotiate freight rates with shippers' councils, which are simply associations of the shippers (as distinguished from the transporters) of cargo. Lastly, pricing structures are often subject to regulation by the governments of either the importing or the exporting country, and sometimes by agreements between the two countries.

39. Intermodalism, which refers to the combination of more than one type of transportation in a single service, got its start when lines found that they achieved a competitive advantage by providing a "door-to-door" service: moving the cargo from the shipper's offices by truck to the train; by train to the port of origin, and hence the ship; and reversing the process at the destination port. It reached its apex, at least for the time being, when American President Lines discovered that it could move containers from the Far East to the U.S. east coast more quickly and cheaply by transhipping them at the west coast to trains than its competitiors could move them directly from the Far East to the U.S. east coast entirely by ship. Its consequent pioneering of the double stack train concept has revolutionized the Far East/U.S. east coast trading pattern. Parenthetically, it is worth noting that intermodalism probably would not have developed to nearly the same degree without the prior development of containerization.

40. For example, strategically adding a port of call may enable the line to fill excess capacity, or dropping a port of call may allow it to raise the level of service to other ports. Also, some lines provide service by chartering container slots on vessels operated by other lines, thus permitting both to benefit. Then again, some lines (and especially the around the world services) attempt to optimize the use of capacity by arranging for local "feeder" services to "feed" them cargo for onshipment at one or more ports along the route.

41. For these purposes, I define capitalization as the sum of stockholders' equity (including preferred stock) and all obligations for borrowed money.

42. The cost of funds in this context includes interest on borrowed funds, and cash dividends on preferred and common stock. Those items that are tax deductible (in most countries, only interest is a tax deductible expense) must be adjusted to reflect that fact by multiplying them by (1-effective tax rate).

43. Actual figures have been divided by a constant.

44. The concept of fixed and variable costs refers to the way that unit costs change with the volume of business done. It is important not to confuse this issue with changes in cost that simply reflect price changes.

45. Financial analysts tend to estimate the average collection period (ACP) by using the following formula:

$$\text{ACP} = \frac{365}{\dfrac{\text{Revenues}}{\text{Receivables}}}$$

One can make a similar calculation for the average accounts payable term (AAPT as follows:

$$\text{AAPT} = \frac{365}{\dfrac{\text{Operating Costs}}{\text{Accounts Payable}}}$$

Both of these calculations are approximations, but if they are significantly differen from normal credit terms, there is a basis for questions.

46. Lenders should not, however, be under any illusion that this kind of financing is only temporary or seasonal. It is truly permanent financing in that receivables collected must sooner or later be replaced by the creation of new receivables. Although in theory a lender should be able to cease making new advances and still be repaid from the collection of the receivables advanced against, it will not be able to do so without impairing the company's ability to do business on an ongoing basis. Further, a lender should bear in mind that short of direct remittance of collections from the agent to the lender, the borrower will be in full control of the flow of funds. Even in the case of direct remittance, if the agent is a "captive" (i.e. wholly owned by the line), or if the line is in a position to influence a contract agent, the line may still be able to control the flow of funds.

47. This is not as simple as it sounds. In the United States, for instance, liens on receivables are typically (especially in states subject to the Uniform Commercial Code) registered in the office of the Secretary of State of the individual states. Theoretically, to be confident that there are no prior liens, a lender should check the records in all fifty states, and also register its own lien in all fifty states. As a practical matter, this is not possible. Lenders attempt to determine the primary places within the U.S. that a line is doing business, and check records/record liens in those states. Even this process may be complicated, if, as is quite common, a line calls at a series of widely dispersed ports, and if one considers the implications of intermodalism.

There is another related issue that lenders should be aware of that pertains to the nationality of the line. Two major banks in the U.S. used to finance the receivables of a Brazilian line, registering their liens as would normally be done in the U.S. The receivables advanced against were mostly those due from major U.S. shippers, and hence posed no particular credit problem. However, Brazilian law governing similar transactions in Brazil gave lenders an automatic lien over all of the line's receivables, and thus it was possible that Brazilian lenders were relying upon the same receivables that the U.S. lenders were relying upon. The receivables were in effect double pledged. Fortunately for all concerned, the issue was never tested, but in a liquidation situation, it certainly would be. For this reason, a prudent lender should check on what bodies of law a line's receivables may be subject to.

48. Any given lender will be primarily interested in the finance ratio for the vessels it has financed, but a fleet finance ratio is useful for anticipating the actions of other lenders.

49. There are a variety of ways to calculate this ratio, depending on what one is trying to learn. I find the ratio of cash flow before interest and taxes to interest plus lease payments plus current maturities of long term debt to be the most useful when analyzing a liner company.

50. There is a tendency among many financial analysts to consider subordinated debt and redeemable preferred stock as categories of equity. With respect to subordinated debt, this is valid only if no principal is due to be repaid until senior obligations have been repaid in full. Also, publicly held subordinated debt may be very difficult to deal with in a workout situation. Likewise there are differing degrees of subordination, which can only be determined by reviewing the related documentation. With respect to redeemable preferred stock, this structurally has more in common with term debt than with equity. Unless it is clear that subordinated debt and redeemable preferred stockholders expect to be repaid by converting their holdings to common shares (as is the case with certain convertible offerings), it is safer to assume that both categories are obligations that will have to be met if the business is to continue on an ongoing basis. Note that the workout situation will also be the situation in which conversion options are unlikely to be exercised.

51. I have never yet seen projections provided by a borrower that did not purport to demonstrate conclusively that the company could meet all its obligations. It is almost as if they had attended a school for borrowers to learn what lenders want to hear. There are strong grounds for believing that they start with the desired results, and work backwards to derive appropriate assumptions.

52. Such as (but not limited to) the *Journal of Commerce, Lloyds List, Fairplay International Shipping Weekly, Seatrade Week,* and *Seatrade Business Review.* Contacts with agents active in a variety of trades are also very useful here.

53. There is no law that says that a lender must offer to provide only what a borrower requested.

54. United States Lines was an excellent example of a multi-ship owning company, while its arch competitor, Evergreen Marine, with its use of flag of convenience vessels, is an excellent example of the other structure.

55. Financing a vessel owned by a special purpose company, with neither a charter nor a corporate guarantee, involves only one clear cut source of repayment: sale of the vessel. Transactions of this sort are always bad lending practice at any level of compensation, except perhaps for a purely speculative investor.

56. U.S. law specifically forbids U.S. residents from trading with certain specified countries, and violations of that law are a criminal as distinct from a civil offense. There is considerable thought that these proscriptions also apply to lenders knowingly financing vessels subject to proscribed charters, and some lenders now habitually include protective language in loan agreements.

57. I am aware of a Brazilian line that is still in existence only because of U.S. dollar advances from its U.S. agent, which the Brazilian line unofficially controls.

58. I have even seen such a case referred to in a bank policy document as "akin to a quasi sovereign risk," which is a gross abuse of the English language.

59. Governments experiencing foreign exchange problems often ban, or at least closely restrict, the ability of domestic companies to maintain bank accounts abroad. In this scenario, the fact that a company earns its own foreign exchange requirements is of little comfort.

Chapter Eight

Documentation of Ship Financing Transactions

Far too often, both borrowers and lenders treat the subject of documentation rather lightly.[1] Sometimes they leave it entirely to their respective attorneys, and provided the matters at issue are technical, or a matter of wording, this is not a problem. However, if the decisions have a commercial impact, both lender and borrower should be directly involved. It is to the advantage of both borrower and lender to fully understand the details of the various agreements. Not only will this protect them in the event of difficulties, but it will also lay the foundation for the smooth operation of the relationship. From this perspective, they should both view the documentation process, tedious as it may be, as an important step in the relationship development process. It is also important for both borrower and lender to use attorneys experienced in this type of transaction, as otherwise the process will not only be inefficient; it will create unnecessary misunderstandings.

Commitment Letter

In the interest of an efficient negotiating process, the starting point in the documentation procedure should always be a commitment letter. A good commitment letter, which is usually drafted by the lender rather than by the lender's attorneys (although perhaps subject to counselor's review), sets forth all the essential terms and conditions of the transaction. It need not contain all the terms and conditions that will ultimately be in the loan agreement, but it should cover all the major financial terms, and all conditions and covenants believed to be in any way critical to the success of the transaction, or in any significant way controversial. Though it is a conditional document in the sense that it is binding only upon completion of additional documents, it is nevertheless legally binding. Courts will hold the requirement for completion of additional documents subject to a test of reasonableness and good faith. It therefore pays to take commitment letters seriously.

Appendix C is an example of a commitment letter for a ship financing.

One of the first issues that must be solved is who the commitment letter should be addressed to. If the prospective borrower is an already established corporate entity, it should, of course, be addressed to that entity. However, if, as is common in this kind of transaction, the borrower will be a not-yet-formed corporate entity, the letter must be addressed to someone else, usually the group's managing agent. However, in this case, the body of the commitment letter must clearly set forth the nature of the obligor; for example, "A to-be-formed Liberian corporation to be established for the sole purpose of purchasing the M/T Vessel."

The first part of the commitment letter should set forth the purpose of the credit facility ("The purchase of the M/T Vessel," or "To refinance an existing $10 million loan from the Export-Import Bank of ________," for example), and the financial terms: amount, amortization schedule, term, interest rate, fees, etc.

The purpose and terms should be closely followed by specification of the security required: mortgages, assignments (include insurance requirements), corporate and/or personal guarantees, and security (if any) for any of the guarantees.

Next should come a listing of essential conditions. There are many possibilities, but typical ones would be proscription of dividends, security maintenance, cash flow recapture, law and jurisdiction, additional documentation, fixture on a time charter at a specified level, and provision for start-up costs.

Last, but not least, a commitment letter should always have an expiry date.

The remainder of the documentation process is based on the commitment letter framework, and usually begins once the borrower has accepted the terms and conditions outlined in the commitment letter.

Loan Agreement

As a general proposition, a loan agreement is a vastly expanded version of the commitment letter. Eurodollar loan agreements, while differing somewhat in structure depending on the firm preparing them, tend to contain certain common basic elements.

To begin with, most agreements include at or near the beginning some variation of a preamble setting forth the interests of the various parties, and their reasons for entering into the transaction. It is worth taking this section seriously, as it is this section that establishes "consideration." "Consideration" is based on the notion that a contract is not enforceable unless it is of clear mutual benefit. Inaccurate or fraudulent statements in a preamble can subsequently be used as an argument against enforceability.

Most agreements include, also at or near the beginning, a definitions section. This section is also worth taking seriously, as errors in this section will be carried throughout the agreement wherever the defined terms are used.

All agreements include one or more sections specifying in detail the necessary drawdown notices; the basis for the calculation of interest; the mechanics and precise timing of payments of principal and interest; provisions for the calculation and payment of interest after an event of default; and the calculation and payment of fees. If the commitment letter was drafted properly, these sections are not usually controversial. Nevertheless, errors in these sections are the most common source of operational difficulties later on.

Usually these sections are closely followed by a section outlining the security required, and a section outlining "conditions precedent." The latter specifies what must happen, and what additional documents must be executed before drawdown will be permitted. Examples would include (but not be limited to) execution, delivery, and registration (where relevant) of a note and all security documents; payment of fees; evidence of the vessel's registration with a clean title; evidence of insurance; evidence that the vessel is "in class"; evidence that the borrower is a corporation in good standing, and that it has taken all necessary steps internally to legally authorize the transaction; and delivery of all relevant legal opinions.

Under most circumstances a borrower should be able to comply with these requirements. However, there are a few exceptions. For instance, there are occasions on which the closing of a vessel purchase must physically take place in one location, while the registration of the mortgage must take place elsewhere. The registration of the mortgage cannot take place without a clean title document from the closing of the purchase, while the closing of the purchase cannot take place without bank financing, which in turn requires mortgage registration as a pre-condition.[2] If one is confident about the financial strength of the borrower and guarantors, one may conclude that the risk of default prior to mortgage registration, or more likely, the risk of another creditor registering a lien that would take preference over the mortgage, is acceptable. Short of that faith, one can only look for some form of additional security to cover the interim risk.

Another problem with security documents is that the charterer's acknowledgement of notice of a charter assignment is often not available prior to drawdown. In any case, a charterer's acknowledgement of the notice is voluntary. As the lack of the acknowledgement does not invalidate the assignment, lenders often choose not to make an issue of it.

As most law firms are unwilling to issue legal opinions until the documents are in final form, and as changes are often being made right up to the closing, the legal opinions are often not available in time. In addition, ship financing transactions often require opinions from a wide variety of jurisdictions, some geographically quite remote.[3] However, drafts of the opinions are usually available, and consequently a lender agreeing to some modest delay adds little to its risk.[4]

Most ship financing loan agreements include a section pertaining to the borrower's bank accounts, and this section will often come shortly after the conditions precedent. This section specifies the application of monies received into the account: that is, the order of priority in which the borrower's payment requirements are to be met. If the assignment of earnings includes provision for a retention account, the operation of this account is set forth here also as the retention payment is usually first in priority. The operation of the retention account, or of the charter hire account if there is no retention account, is particularly sensitive. Errors in this area can be costly for both borrower and lender, and the order in which other payment claims are to be met is also rather critical. Usually the agreement specifies that monies should be applied first to amounts other than principal and interest that are due under the security documents;[5] then to payment of accrued interest on the loan; then to payments of principal; and last to whosoever is entitled to the remaining balance, usually the owner (i.e. to the operating account) for use in the day to day operations of the business.

Most agreements include a section labelled "Representations and Warranties." Because of their direct relationship to conditions precedent, representations and warranties may be placed in close proximity to the conditions precedent section, but this is not necessarily the case. In any case, this section is designed to set forth various assumptions, which if found to be invalid, would deter the lender from advancing the loan. For example, the borrower must represent that it is duly incorporated, with full power to carry on the business contemplated; that it is the legal owner of the vessel; that the vessel has a clean title, except for mortgages securing indebtedness to be refinanced; that it has the legal power and authority to enter into the transaction, and the obligations assumed will be legally binding; that all consents and authorizations of relevant governmental authorities and agencies necessary to make the security documents enforceable have been obtained; that it is not in default under any agreement to which it is a party, and it is not subject to any material[6] litigation or governmental administrative proceedings; that information previously provided was accurate and that there has been no material adverse change since the date of that information; the charter (if there is one) is in full force and effect; and that no event that would be an event of default has occurred and is continuing. This long, but nevertheless not exhaustive list, is heavily oriented toward the legal enforceability of the agreement. The legal opinions required as a condition precedent are intended to provide evidenciary support for enforceability. The significance of the representations is self-evident, as any one of them could be used to set aside the agreement.[7]

The next major issue to be addressed in most loan agreements is that of covenants. Often but not always these are sub-divided into affirmative and negative covenants. Typical affirmative covenants include the borrower's obligations to conduct its business in a responsible manner; provide financial and other data within an agreed time frame; comply with all relevant laws and government regulations; use the proceeds of the loan for their intended purpose; inform the lender of the happening of events of default and perform all its obligations under the charter, charter and lease assignments, and mortgage.

Typical negative convenants include the borrower's promises not to allow its assets to be encumbered with liens, or to take action within an agreed period of time to cause any such liens to be lifted; not to borrow additional monies except on a subordinated basis; not to make loans or advances to third parties; not to engage in business other than ownership and operation of the ship; not to guarantee obligations incurred by third parties; not to pay dividends; and not to permit any change in its ownership.

These lists of typical covenants, neither of which is exhaustive, must, of course, be tailored to the requirements of each specific situation. They are intended to clearly establish the basis upon which business will be conducted. They do not, however, by themselves, give the lender any rights to a course of action. The basis for a course of action is set by specifying events of default, which are usually the subject of the next section of the loan agreement.

Typical events of default (again, not an exhaustive list) are the borrower's failure to make payments when due; failure to observe the covenants; incorrect or inaccurate representations and warranties; default on other debt of the same or affiliated companies; receivership, bankruptcy, or general assignment for the benefit of creditors; and failure to comply with, or invalidity of the security documents. Specification of events of default would be useless without specification of appropriate remedies, and the loan agreement sets these forth as well, sometimes in the events of default section, and sometimes in a separate section. The principal remedy is to declare the indebtedness immediately due and payable, and to foreclose on the vessel. However, most loan agreements recognize that events of default vary in level of seriousness and therefore allow the borrower an agreed period of time to cure them in appropriate cases.

Most Eurodollar loan agreements contain a section or sections often loosely referred to as Eurodollar disaster provisions. Such provisions contemplate the theoretical possibility that the Eurodollar market could fall apart, and that as a result, the lender might be unable to continue to fund itself in U.S. dollars, or might be unable to determine the LIBOR rate. Generally speaking, such provisions call for negotiations in good faith between the borrower and the lender with view to finding an alternative funding source or an alternative method of determining the interest rate. Should these negotiations fail, however, the provisions typically call for the borrower to prepay the loan.

On the surface, it might appear unreasonable to a borrower to be held responsible for a funding problem over which it has no control. Such provisions are a relic of the early days of the Eurodollar market, when funding availability had not really been tested by significant adverse circumstances. Indeed, in the early 1970's, lenders used to worry that one significant default on a Eurodollar loan might cause the Eurodollar market to collapse. Today, lenders seeing that the Eurodollar market has experienced geometric growth despite the impact of oil price cartels, accumulations of dollar holdings by oil producing nations, and massive loan defaults by developing countries, may be tempted to agree that the concern is academic. In any case, disaster clauses continue to be standard practice, and in any unforeseen crisis situation, could serve a useful purpose in forcing the parties to the agreement to negotiate in good faith. Certainly a forced prepayment would be in neither party's best interest; prepayment from the borrower's own funds would be likely to require an extraordinary degree of liquidity, and failure to prepay would be likely to force a foreclosure under the least favorable of circumstances. Similarly, the circumstances that caused the market to collapse would make it difficult or impossible for the borrower to refinance the loan with another lender.

Sometimes mixed in with the Eurodollar disaster provisions, and sometimes set forth separately, are so-called increased cost provisions. The concept here is usually easier for borrowers to accept. Generally speaking, they provide that if any change in law, taxation (other than taxes on the lender's overall net income), or government regulation (such as imposition of reserve requirements) has the effect of increasing the lender's cost of funding the loan, the interest shall be adjusted to compensate. Usually such provisions also give the borrower the right to prepay the loan in the event of such an adjustment, as the factors giving rise to the increased costs may not effect all lenders equally, and therefore the borrower may be able to refinance the loan at a lower cost.[8]

There are two other common features of Eurodollar loan agreements worthy of comment. The first is the concept of a judgment currency clause, which makes good sense to the lender, but is far from universally included. A judgment currency clause attempts to provide against the event that the lender is forced to arrest the ship in a port in which the currency of the loan is different from the local currency. In this event, local courts, assuming they agree to enforce the lender's claim, may allow the cash proceeds of the sale to be payable to the lender only in local currency. If the country in question regulates the exchange of this local currency for the currency of the loan, the lender's actual collection of the judgment funds may be delayed. If exchange rates move unfavorably in meantime, the lender may incur a loss. The judgment currency clause would require the borrower to compensate the lender for that loss.

The second common feature is the appointment of an agent for service of process. When the borrower and the lender are not located conveniently to each other, it is common practice in loan agreements to require the borrower to appoint an agent in the lender's jurisdiction upon whom notices can be served with the same force and effect as if they had been served directly upon the borrower. When the borrower is a company incorporated in another country, such as Liberia or Panama, appointment of such an agent becomes especially critical. If the vessel's managing agent is appropriately located, it may be appointed as agent for service of process. Otherwise, the agent for service of process may be any third party appropriately located. Sometimes a borrower's attorneys are willing to serve in this capacity, but there are also companies, such as C.T. Corporation Systems in New York that make a business of serving in this capacity for a fee.

The Note

In any lending transaction, the primary evidence of indebtedness is a note.[9] The note is typically a short document which, when duly signed by authorized officers of the borrower, formally acknowledges the indebtedness. In most cases, it also reiterates the principal terms of the indebtedness (interest rate, amortization, repayment terms, etc.), and incorporates the loan agreement and security documents by reference. In general, it is very difficult to enforce the terms of a loan agreement in the absence of a note[10], and therefore it it perhaps the most critical single document underlying the transaction. Lenders should be very careful to safeguard it until the loan has been fully repaid.

The Mortgage

Marine mortgages have two distinct though related purposes. In the first instance, they serve as evidence of a lien on the vessel. That lien must be officially recorded with an agency or representative of the government of the "flag state".[11] Recording of the mortgage, usually evidenced by a stamp of the authority recording it, showing (among other things) the date and time of recording, serves as a public record of the lien. As such, it is vital evidence of the lien should enforcement ever be necessary. Likewise, it is the means by which creditors in general can determine the degree to which the vessel is subject to prior claims. Last, but not least, it is evidence of the priority of the lien, as typically liens will be enforced in the order in which they were recorded[12] (hence the importance of the date and time stamps).

The second purpose of mortgages is to serve as an agreement between the borrower and the lender with respect to the mainenance, insurance, and manner of operation of the vessel.

Some mortgages, particularly those done under English law, and those of countries whose legal systems had their basis in English law, explicitly recognize the distinction between the two purposes of mortgages by requiring two separate documents. The lien is recorded by way of a short (usually two page) "boiler plate" document to which is attached a separate, much longer document (a deed of covenant) that is the agreement between borrower and lender (who of course is also the mortgagee). Most mortgages, however, carry out both purposes in a single document.

The mortgage language that serves to register the lien and make it enforceable is usually determined by the body of applicable law, and is seldom negotiable or even controversial. Since it is usually "boiler plate," it can usually be left to attorneys without borrower and lender getting involved. The deed of covenant (or the equivalent in a mortgage serving both purposes), however, is not "boiler plate", and because it covers so many aspects of a vessel's operations, it is worthwhile for both lender and borrower to scrutinize it and negotiate it carefully.

Deeds of covenant (or the equivalent) tend to cover a number of common issues, regardless of the flag state.[13]

First, as with the loan agreement, it pays to give special attention to the definitions section, as any errors here will be carried throughout the document.

Second, it usually makes sense to review the section that specifies exactly what is being mortgaged. Usually this is rather all-encompassing, but an omission, even though inadvertent, can be an opening for another creditor to take precedence, at least in part.[14]

Third, most if not all mortgages have a section relating to insurance cover, specifying the amounts and types of cover that must be carried, and entitling the lender to arrange such cover should the owner fail to do so. The owner also typically agrees not to trade or employ the vessel otherwise than in accordance with the terms of the insurance without first obtaining the consent of the underwriters and paying any additional premium that the underwriters require.

To appreciate the significance of this last provision one only has to consider the prospect of tankers that trade into and out of the Arabian Gulf, with all the dangers they face from attack from the military forces of both Iraq and Iran. Unfortunately, if the owner decides to trade into an area requiring special agreement by the underwriters without making special insurance arrangements, there is nothing the lender can do retrospectively to protect the value of its collateral. If it knows in advance where the vessel is going, it can, of course, arrange the special cover if the owner fails to do so. As a practical matter, though, few lenders keep such close track of a mortgaged vessel's movements unless they suspect improper trading, or are planning to arrest the vessel. Lenders tend to rely instead for protection on a mutuality of interest in preserving the employability of the vessel.[15]

Fourth, most if not all, mortgages also have a section relating to operation and maintenance. This will include such obvious covenants as keeping the vessel in a good state of repair; keeping the vessel in compliance with its classification society standards; furnishing information to the lender; reimbursing the lender for amounts it advances on behalf of the owner; giving the lender the right to physically inspect the vessel; and maintaining registration of the vessel under an acceptable flag, and in compliance with flag regulations.

Some other covenants are less obvious, but nevertheless important. For example, usually the owner agrees not to employ the vessel in any illegal trade or business. The danger is that the vessel could be seized and/or condemned or destroyed, and that insurance cover might be invalidated. Again, the owner usually agrees to promptly pay all tolls, dues, and other vessel or voyage expenses, the danger being that any such sums outstanding could result in the creation of liens ranking prior to the mortgage.[16] Similarly, the owner typically covenants to ensure that if any liens arise, they will be removed within an agreed time frame.[17] It is worth noting that such liens can be a double edged sword: not only may they rank prior to the mortgage, but as long as the underlying obligation has not been paid or (if the claim is disputed) bail provided,[18] the vessel will in all likelihood be prevented from leaving the port in which the lien was imposed, and may even be arrested. Until it can once again trade freely, it will earn no hire, with all that that implies for its ability to service debt.

Last, but not least, this section sets forth the lender's requirements for physically evidencing the mortgage on board the ship. Typically, this means that a certified copy of the mortgage must be included with the ship's papers, and notices of mortgage posted conspicuously in the chart room and the master's cabin.[19] The purpose, of course, is to put other potential creditors on notice of the lender's claim.

Fifth, like loan payments, mortgages specify events of default. Generally speaking, these include failure to comply with any of the covenants specified in the mortgage, plus all events of default in the loan agreement. Equally importantly, however, they set out in detail the lender's remedies with respect to the mortgaged vessel. These vary somewhat depending on the laws of the flag country, but normally include taking physical possession of the vessel; taking control of insurance records; collecting or negotiating any outstanding claims; discharging and/or negotiating other liens; selling the vessel; and managing, insuring, maintaining, and employing the vessel. For these purposes, the document grants the lender the owner's power of attorney and provides that if the vessel is sold, the purchaser need not enquire as to whether the sale was within the lender's legal power.

One last issue usually addressed in mortgages, and often a point of contention in the negotiating process, is that of the application of proceeds. This issue arises in two forms. First, with respect to payment of insurance claims, it is customary to provide that all amounts in excess of a specified threshold amount be paid by the underwriters directly to the lender. Contention occasionally arises over the choice of the threshold amount: owners typically wish to set it at a high level, while lenders prefer to set it at a lower level. Second, it is customary to set forth how the proceeds of any sale of the vessel will be applied, and in what order. Usually, this will be first to any amounts advanced on the owner's behalf; second to interest; third to loan principal; and the remaining balance (if any) to the owner.

The Assignment of Insurance/Earnings

One basic principle of lending is that a simple lien, in the absence of a related security agreement, will generally be unenforceable. As noted above, the marine mortgage may combine the lien and the security agreement in one document. In contrast, the various assignments of insurances, reinsurances (if such there be) and earnings are security agreements only. The registration of the lien(s) is accomplished separately.

In contrast to loan agreements and sometimes mortgages, the texts of assignment agreements are rarely controversial. The key to them is that the borrower (usually referred to in the agreement as ''Assignor'') covenants to do certain things. The most important of these is to instruct the insurance underwriters, reinsurers and/or insurance broker to incorporate a loss payable clause in the policies. It also specifies the contents of that clause, and this is worth some attention, as it is this clause that defines the flow of funds when insurance claims are paid.

To begin with, the loss payable clause notes the lender's interest in the proceeds of insurance claims. The clause also defines when claims are to be paid to the borrower and when directly to the lender, and in the latter case, may even specify an account to which the payments are to be made. Furthermore, loss payable clauses specify notices that the underwriters must give to the lender before cancelling or failing to renew the policies. The obvious intent is to give the lender the opportunity to correct any events of default under the policies, the most common one being non-payment of premium or (in the cast of P&I clubs, call).

The inclusion of loss payable clauses in insurance contracts is standard practice, and underwriters and brokers seldom balk at doing so.[20] While copies of the contracts with the loss payable clause incorporated are seldom physically available at loan closings, usually the underwriters or brokers are in a position to confirm in writing or by telex that the clause has been added. It is important to understand that the loss payable clause, once incorporated in the policy, is legally binding upon the underwriter(s), and therefore a lender can feel quite comfortable proceeding with the loan even though the policy with the clause incorporated is not physically available. As a matter of prudence, however, it should require that a copy be made available within a reasonable period of time (three weeks?).

Assignments of earnings are similar in concept to assignments of insurance, but in most cases, somewhat less complex. The basic issue is that the borrower covenants to notify its charterers that the charter has been assigned, and that hire should be paid directly to the lender. Sometimes the assignment also specifies an account (the charterhire account) to which the charterhire is to be paid, and this information should always be included in the notice to the charterer. This is particularly the case when the document is a general assignment of charters to be entered into in the future rather than the assignment of a specific charter.[21]

The assignment of earnings will always include some variation of a notice to the charterer. For the reasons described in Chapter VII, the agreement depends on the cooperation of the charterer, and hence in the absence of an acknowledgement may be difficult to enforce. The notice should at least be sent, as absent notice to the charterer, it will be difficult to build even the outlines of a legally enforceable claim.

The rules and procedures for registering the relevant liens pertaining to the assignment agreements vary widely from jurisdiction to jurisdiction. In some cases (frequently with insurance assignments) there is no way at all to record such liens with public authorities. In the United States, in states that have adopted the Uniform Commercial Code it is customary to make UCC-1[22] filings, at least over the borrower's bank accounts. Competent attorneys will know how to go about this.

The Pledge of Shares

Some ship financings call for the borrower's shareholders to pledge their shares in the borrowing company as additional security. This gives the lender some additional flexibility in event of default, as instead of going through arrest and foreclosure proceedings, it can replace the company officers with officers responsible solely to it, and operate or sell the ship in an orderly manner. As a practical matter, however, there are apt to be a number of legal constraints and or risks associated with a lender's attempt to exercise its rights under the pledge.[23] Overall, from a lender's perspective, it is probably better to have a pledge than not to have it, and a borrower (at least a borrower that is a single purpose company) usually has little to lose by granting it.

The terms of the share pledge agreement are seldom particularly controversial. Occasionally, the borrower's shareholders attempt to limit which events of default can result in the lender's exercising its rights. Sometimes the shareholders attempt to write into the agreement some provisions defining procedures designed to ensure that the lender maximizes the value of the borrower's corporate assets. Lastly, the shareholders sometimes request that they be given a first refusal to buy the shares if the shares themselves are sold. Usually, there is little difficulty successfully negotiating these issues.

Generally speaking, there is no need to register a lien over the shares. The shareholders put the shares in the lender's physical possession, and provided the lender also holds the stockpowers, there should be no difficulty enforcing the claim. Furthermore, the lender will find that the exercise of its rights proceeds more smoothly if it also holds the undated resignations of the corporate officers.

Guarantees

Some guarantees, because of the specific nature of a transaction, include covenants and provisions of the sort applicable to a borrower, and to the extent that this is so, they will require a certain amount of negotiation. Otherwise, though, there are three principal issues that seem to arise on a regular basis. These are severability, guarantee of payment versus guarantee of collection, and right of subrogation.

The severability issue arises when there is more than one guarantor, and the guarantors are not affiliated. If a transaction involves a joint venture of multiple unaffiliated shareholders, they may wish to guarantee only the same proportion of the amounts guaranteed as they own of the borrower's shares. The lender would typically prefer for all guarantors to assume responsibility for the total amount guaranteed. The resolution of the issue depends on the relative negotiating strengths of the various parties to the transaction. It is worth noting that a guarantor's perception of the issue may be colored by the terms of the joint venture agreement and/or shareholder's agreement, and it consequently behooves the lender to be aware of these terms. If the partners are individually financially strong, then there is no great risk in accepting several guarantees. Problems may arise, though, if one or more of the partners is significantly weaker than the other(s). The only foolproof solution is to require joint and several guarantees, in which all of the guarantors guarantee the full amount. However, one may still find reason to accept several guarantees if the total transaction risk is otherwise acceptable, the lender recognizes the relative weaknesses of the partners, and the rewards reflect the higher degree of risk involved.

Borrowers/guarantors often attempt to induce lenders to accept guarantees that are guarantees of collection, but not of payment. The former requires the lender to exhaust all possible remedies against the borrower and its assets before making claim under the guarantee. The latter only requires notice and claim. The former is clearly very disadvantageous to a lender, and if a lender makes a decision to accept it,[24] it should insist upon appropriate additional compensation.

The issue of subrogation is important, but not usually controversial. It refe
to the relative rights of the lender and the guarantor(s) vis a vis the borrower
assets. The lender typically wishes to ensure that it does not lose its righ
until the obligations to it have been fully satisfied. By the same token, th
guarantor, so as to minimize its losses under the guarantee, wishes to establis
its claim on the borrower's assets as quickly as possible. In fact, guarante
typically are based on the assumption that the lender's rights will pass mo
or less automatically to the guarantor once the guaranteed obligations hav
been fully satisfied, but it is well to be explicit on this point. Usually the
is little difficulty finding mutually acceptable language.

In addition to the foregoing, there are a few issues of lesser importance. Firs
it is important to be clear that the guarantee applies not just to amounts du
under the loan agreement, but also to all other amounts, such as legal fe
and out of pocket expenses, amounts advanced to the master to cov
operating costs, or amounts advanced to pay insurance premiums, that ma
be due under the security documents.

Second, the language in personal guarantees is much the same as for corpora
guarantees, but the conditions precedent are apt to be quite different, as the
is no corporate good standing to be established.

Third, if appropriate, a lender may take security for a guarantor's obligatio
under the guarantee agreement. In fact, this is often the only way
accomplish cross collateralization. In most cases, the relevant documentatio
follows the same pattern as the documentation for the security related
the loan.

Notes

1. I even remember an occasion when an experienced New York money center ban
on the date of drawdown, did not even have a note, much less a mortgage, lo
agreement, or other security documents.

2. This situation is not merely hypothetical. I once financed a vessel for which th
closing of the purchase took place in London. However, the vessel was to fly th
Singapore flag, and be subject to a Singapore mortgage. Unlike a Liberian mortgag
which with appropriate arrangements with Liberian Services, Inc. can be register
almost anywhere, a Singapore mortgage could be registered only in Singapore. Becau
I only had to make a partial advance at closing, and because I was also taking
mortgage over a Panamanian flag vessel for which mortgage registration was n
a problem, I felt comfortable allowing the borrower a few days to register th
Singapore mortgage. This was actually done after the first loan advance had bee
made.

. Visualize a loan agreement written under the laws of England, vessel mortgages
ıder the laws of Liberia, Panama, and Singapore, and corporate guarantors
corporated in the State of Delaware and the Canton of Zug (Switzerland), with
ch jurisdiction requiring its own legal opinion, and the dimensions of the problem
come much clearer. This situation is also not merely hypothetical.

. I am not convinced that legal opinions add much to the solidity of financial
cumentation. It is, of course, important to be aware of possible legal issues, but
e draft opinions usually suffice for this purpose. Most legal opinions are heavily
alified in their scope, and in any case, take note of even the most hypothetical
gal risks. It is therefore very difficult to hold a firm issuing an opinion responsible
r anything other than the gravest and most obvious of errors.

. This refers to the fact that the security documents normally permit the lender
its sole option to meet various obligations of the borrower, such as insurance
emiums and crew wages, if the borrower is unable to. Such sums become additional
nounts due under the security documents, and these amounts due are also secured.

. The concept of materiality occurs over and over in ship financing documentation.
documentation as complex as this, it would be easy for either borrower or lender
take advantage of technicalities to its own advantage. The materiality test is intended
avoid this problem. Unfortunately, the concept does not have an objective meaning,
d hence it cannot be relied upon.

. From a lender's perspective, the danger is less from the borrower (although this
k cannot be dismissed) than from a receiver or a court attempting to stretch assets
insufficient value to meet multiple obligations.

. Whether or not it is in the borrower's interest to do so depends on the remaining
nount and term of the loan, the interest rate differential resulting, and the transaction
sts (prepayment fees, facility fees, legal fees, etc.) associated with the refinancing.
simple present value analysis of the relevant cash flows should clarify the issue.

. With respect to standby letters of credit, the primary evidence of the obligation
the standby letter of credit application form. With respect to bank guarantees, the
uivalent document is usually a counter guarantee agreement.

. Historically, many Eurodollar loan agreements written so as to be subject to
glish law have forgone the use of notes. The theory is that as the loan agreement
registered with the Companies House, a note is not necessary. In recent years,
wever, it has become increasingly common for even English law loan agreements
make use of notes. In any country but England, it would be foolish to forego the
of a note, but even there, it is definitely better to have it than not to have it.

. The nationality of the mortgage is usually determined by the vessel's flag rather than the borrower's country of incorporation. Not all flag states require that vessels flying their flag be owned by companies incorporated in the flag state. Much of the Greek flag fleet, for example, is owned by companies incorporated in Liberia and Panama.

12. In most jurisdictions, certain claims will routinely be held to rank ahead of al recorded liens. I will elaborate on this subject in Chapter X.

13. The ensuing discussion uses the Liberian mortgage as a model, but that does no make the commentary any less relevant for other mortgages.

14. This may seem hypothetical, but I remember at least one transaction that wa predicated on mortgaging a vessel's engines separately from the remainder of the ship In the end, the transaction was not completed, but significantly, the prospectiv lender's attorneys believed that the concept was legally viable.

15. Absent financial difficulties, the mutuality of interest can probably be safely relie upon. However, it is not difficult to envisage a situation in which a financially trouble owner deliberately trades a vessel into a dangerous area in order to take advantag of the higher freight rates attainable there (the higher freight rates themselves ten to reflect the higher insurance premiums required). By not actually paying the highe premium, he receives a cash windfall. The success of such a trading decision depends of course, on his not having to make a claim, as the underwriters will justifiably refus to pay, and both owner and lender will suffer the consequences.

16. The prior ranking of such claims arises because of the in rem versus in person concept in maritime law. I will elaborate further on this subject in Chapter X.

17. This agreed time frame is often a point of contention when the borrower an the lender negotiate the documentation. The former always wants the longest possibl time, and the latter wants the shortest possible time. In my experience, fifteen day is usually adequate, but I have seen up to thirty days allowed.

18. If the owner posts the amount of bail required by the local court, in effe providing security for the disputed claim, the vessel will usually be released. Bail ca take the form of cash, but owners usually prefer to arrange for their P&I club t issue a bond. Given either cash security or a standby letter of credit from the owner bank, most P&I clubs are willing and able to provide this service.

19. It is very difficult to enforce this requirement, short of physical inspection. Or of the closing documents is usually a notice to the vessel's master, requiring him t comply, and to certify that he has complied. This notice, however, cannot be issue until after the closing, and therefore certification must be after the fact. Given th in most cases the loan has already been disbursed, there is no convenient way fc the lender to exert pressure towards compliance.

20. Sometimes P&I clubs object to what seem to them to be the onerous requirements of loss payable clauses, and propose an alternative, less stringent text. While lenders would usually prefer the stricter text, the clause is less critical than in the case of hull and machinery and war risks coverage. Furthermore, as a practical matter, lenders and borrowers have little leverage with which to force the issue, and therefore they usually accept the alternative language.

1. If the vessel is subject to a time charter that expires before the final maturity of the loan, the documentation may include both specific and general assignments.

2. UCC-1's are a standard form used in the United States for registering liens in tates subject to the Uniform Commercial Code. They are filed with a competent ublic authority (usually the Secretary of State of the relevant state) which date/time tamps them, thus establishing the priority of the lien. There are two issues concerning JCC-1 filings worth noting. First, their validity is limited to five years. If the term f the extension of credit exceeds five years, they must be refiled, preferably about ix months before they expire (the six month advance refiling is intended to preclude charge of fraudulent preference: see below). Second, if a UCC-1 is filed less than ix months prior to bankruptcy, a court may hold that the borrower granted the lien ith knowledge that its bankruptcy was imminent. The bankruptcy court may rule hat under these circumstances, the borrower had fraudulently given preference to ne creditor over another, and such "fraudulent preference" will be the basis for nvalidating the lender's apparently prior claim, and demoting it to the status of an nsecured creditor. On the other hand, once the six months have passed without ankruptcy occurring, the lien may be considered "perfected," or theoretically nchallengeable.

3. The principal constraint will usually be the laws concerning shareholder rights, nd these vary widely depending on the body of corporate law applying to the urisdiction of incorporation. Generally speaking, however, it is clear that the hareholders have an obvious vested interest in seeing that the maximum possible alue is realized from the corporate assets. If a lender exercises its rights under a hare pledge, many courts will nevertheless enforce, according to their best lights, he shareholders' right to asset value maximization. What the court enforces may ot be in what the lender perceives as its best interest. At the very least, the additional exibility expected may not actually be achieved.

he risk aspect of a lender's exercising its right under a share pledge has not yet been riously tested. It involves the issue of "lender liability", a concept limited so far the United States. The essential concept is that if a lender can be construed to ontrol a borrower's operations (as one might expect to see happen if the borrower ere in default), it opens itself up to being held responsible for other of the borrower's abilities.

o far, the application of this concept has been limited to liabilities for the cost of eanup of hazardous waste disposal sites, but given the nature of lawmaking and igation in the U.S., I would not be surprised to see the concept expanded. Imagine, r example, that a tanker being operated by a bank after having exercised its rights

under the share pledge, is caught dumping its slops from tank cleaning in U.S. water
Responsibility for the cleanup costs and fines would fall first on the owning compan
but if its resources were inadequate, it is not difficult to see how the concept cou
be extended to make the bank responsible.

24. I have never accepted a guarantee of collection only, and would be very relucta
to do so. Such arrangements are likely to make workouts out of transactions th
otherwise need not be workouts. Those who have had no workout experience w
have difficulty understanding the significance of this fact. While the legal and ou
of-pocket expenses (and these are extensive in workouts) would be recoverable fro
the borrower and/or guarantors, the demands on and cost of lending officer ar
management time are not, and will almost always greatly outweigh any margin
benefits.

Chapter Nine

Ship Financing for Owners in Developing Countries

s noted in Chapter I, shipowners in developing countries will find it difficult the extreme to achieve their fleet growth objectives in the absence of direct :cess to the international ship financing community. The ship financing ›mmunity today is very reluctant to extend credit to shipowners with a long ack record of operations, demonstrated financial substance, and residency a country without any foreign exchange difficulties. The developing country iipowner's problems are compounded. Its operations may have been recently tablished, resulting in an insufficiently long track record; it may be able demonstrate financial substance, but highly inflationary environments may ake this substance very difficult to assess; and its operations may be plagued / a problem not of its own creation, namely foreign exchange controls. As these obstacles were not enough, many developing countries decided at e governmental level to pursue fleet expansion policies without putting in ace the necessary legal infrastructure: particularly viable flag regulations; mortgage that provides real protection to foreign lenders; and a body of ›ntract law that meets international standards. These issues were previously scussed in Chapter Seven.

would be nice to believe that anywhere there is a problem, there is a lution, or perhaps even an opportunity. This is true at least to some degree th respect to shipowners in developing countries.

ne key is for the owner to develop a mindset and style of doing business at is truly international, as distinguished from relating only to the import/export or cabotage business of its own country. This means building an international reputation for competent vessel operations; deliberately seeking out business with clients in other countries so as to acquire an independent source of foreign exchange that may be assigned to prospective lenders; investing in modern tonnage that meets international standards, even if that means slower fleet growth; and developing a business structure that will make it possible to borrow or otherwise raise the necessary capital. A corollary to this will be to go as far as possible to create a legal environment that foreign lenders and investors can live with.

The track record issue (if such there be) can be addressed in two ways. The first (and best) is to leverage on the longer track record and experience of others until such time as the track record can stand on its own. The usual way to do this is to enter into joint ventures with foreign shipowners with longer experience and track records.

Joint ventures, it must be admitted, are an imperfect solution. First, they suffer from all the strains and stresses of any partnership, but with the added complication of major cultural differences. Second, the motivation of the developed country partner may be suspect. Often it is correctly perceived by the developing country partner as being only interested in obtaining locally available special benefits, such as cargo preference or bunker subsidies. The developing country partner will wish to ensure that it receives real benefits, such as training and marketing assistance, rather than merely serving as a front for the foreigner; and that it will not get stuck permanently in a junior management role. Otherwise, it will never achieve an independent track record. By the same token, the developing country partner must acknowledge that the other partner will require a real economic benefit from the association. It will be vital for the developing country partner to recognize that shipowners in most developed countries rely much more heavily on the terms of a written contract than would be normal in, for instance, Latin America. Thus, it will be important for its own benefit to ensure that the respective responsibilities and economic rewards are clearly set forth in writing, and then steadfastly abided by.

Joint ventures also suffer from one other glaring deficiency, which is the intended transitory nature of the association. There is little reason for a developed country shipowner to enter into the relationship at all unless there is tangible economic benefit. This might take the form of cargo preference or bunker subsidies, or of access to a market otherwise foreclosed. It might also take the form of employment for vessels that otherwise could not be as profitably employed. Seldom will consultancy fees or dividends from a permanent minority investment be sufficient by themselves, and in the consultancy fees case, may even represent a conflict of interest. There is therefore a major incentive for the developed country partner to seek to maximize its rewards while short-changing its responsibilities.

Despite all these difficulties, there are times when a joint venture makes the most sense. However, a better way is to associate by contract with experienced entities that lack the inherent conflicts of interest that go with an association with another shipowner. For example, with respect to technical matters and physical management of vessels, it would be better to associate with a professional ship management company. Such companies usually have more than the usual flexibility to adjust their staffing levels, and within limits, are less concerned with the temporary nature of the relationship. The good ones are willing to contemplate integrating all or part of the staff of the shipowner's company into their own organizations on a temporary basis, simultaneously accomplishing the desired training and minimizing the impact of the temporary nature of the relationship on staffing level fluctuations. Parenthetically, it is worth emphasizing the importance of associating only with a manager of excellent reputation, even if the cost is higher. There are many ways that a professional manager can take financial advantage of a client. Association with a substandard manager may result in financial loss, and, adding insult to injury, the owner may become tarred by the brush of the manager's inferior reputation. Once again, it is worth emphasizing the importance of clearly setting forth in writing and understanding all the terms of the contract.

With respect to marketing, association with a vessel operating pool is probably preferable to direct association with another shipowner. In this scenario, the vessel(s) will have to meet the specifications and operating standards of the pool. This may be useful discipline and learning experience, and can be accomplished with the assistance of a competent professional vessel manager (note that a pool manager also serving as vessel manager has an inherent conflict of interest, and hence such an arrangement should be avoided). It is worth once again reiterating the importance of the reputation of the pool manager and the terms of the contract. It is also worth considering secondment of a trusted employee to the pool manager's organization for the duration of the contract to look after the owner's interest.

In the case of a liner company, contract agents can serve the same purpose as the pool manager.

The second way to offset the track record problem is to arrange financing under the umbrella of a bank or government guarantee. In theory, such an arrangement buys time to develop a track record, but since taken by itself it provides no mechanism for training and development, it is hard to see any lasting value. Perhaps it could work in conjunction with association with professional vessel and pool managers, but unfortunately it suffers from two other major deficiencies. First, from a lender's perspective it relieves the owner of any incentive to perform to a financial standard. Second, from the perspective of both owner and lender, it throws the risk analysis back into the problems of sovereign risk discussed in Chapter VII, which may actually result in foreclosure of access to financing sources that might otherwise be available (see further on). Likewise, government support is likely to result in government restrictions having no relationship to economic reality, and may well end up being counterproductive.

The issue of financial substance is more difficult. To the extent that a lender is being asked to rely on shipping assets employed internationally (and hence generally earning a U.S. dollar, or other convertible currency income stream) it should be in a position to assess their value. To the extent that financial strength depends on assets held locally, denominated in local currency, and not saleable abroad, it is probably unreasonable to expect international lenders to rely on them. If the shipowner has shipping or non-shipping assets held outside his own country, these may be used to support the credit. Unfortunately, the use of such assets in this way, and perhaps even their existence is apt to be politically sensitive.[1]

The foregoing relates to qualitative considerations in assessing financial substance. It is also worth considering the quantitative issue, namely how much substance is enough?[2]

Financial substance is traditionally defined in terms of "net worth", "net assets", or some variation on the theme of the difference between assets and liabilities. There is no magic answer to how much is enough. The answer tends to depend less on any objective standard than on the financing institution's own capitalization and marketing strategy. Some large institutions, for example, seek to make their profits by lending large amounts to large owners, on the assumption that this is the most efficient use of their capital. Others, including both large and medium sized banks, have preferred a "niche" strategy. By getting to know the requirements and solving the problems of a particular market sector, banks seek to influence pricing in that market sector, thus enhancing the return on the business. Banks following this strategy may be willing to consider smaller transactions with smaller owners. To date, only a handful of banks have made a serious effort to actively seek developing country ship finance. These banks exhibit no particular size pattern, but in only one case does such business constitute a major portion of its volume.

In sum, quality does not depend on size, but size will probably make it easier to attract a lender's interest. Because of its large capital requirements, ship financing business tends to be concentrated in large banks. A developing country shipowner will be best served by seeking out a bank that makes or can be induced to make the shipowner's country a market niche.[3]

The business structure and legal infrastructure issues are closely interrelated. The ideal would be to influence the relevant governmental authorities to implement the necessary body of laws and flag regulations, the key issue being the ability of a mortgagee, whether foreign or domestic, to quickly foreclose and realize value by selling the vessel in the international market if the loan is in default. With respect to flag regulations, the key issues are the elimination of all restrictions on cross trading, and of regulations that create a comparative cost disadvantage. For example, regulations that require all insurance to be placed through a government agency or company serve only to artificially increase premiums with no improvement in the quality of the cover (which is ultimately reinsured in the international market anyway). Likewise, regulations that require higher levels of crewing than are operationally necessary only serve counterproductive purposes.

Efforts to change the legal infrastructure take one into the political arena, and unfortunately, shipowners outside of traditional maritime countries tend to be a rather small political constituency. Therefore, in most cases, such efforts, if worthwhile at all, must be expected to yield results only in the long run. This is not a problem peculiar to developing countries: one of the major problems of the U.S. flag is that the regulatory environment is a political nightmare.

There are three principal ways of dealing with the legal infrastructure problem. The first two do not address any flag regulation questions. They are dual registry and finance leases.

The usual form taken by dual registry is ownership by a company incorporated in a jurisdiction with a mortgage law meeting international standards, thus giving the lender acceptable protection. The vessel is then bareboat chartered to a company in the owner's country, entitling it to fly that flag. The largest number of transactions of this sort that have been done have involved Panama (acceptable mortgage) and the Philippines, but Panama/Mexico, Panama/Chile and others have also been done. Vanuatu (acceptable mortgage) is in the process of implementing a relevant body of law, and Liberia (acceptable mortgage) is an obvious candidate to work with African countries.

The dual registry concept has not yet been adequately tested under adverse circumstances, but there are three concerns that bankers and lawyers share to some degree. First, dual registration arrangements can become politically sensitive in the bareboat charter state, especially if there is any appearance of abuse. For example, the Philippines' authorities have become concerned of late that some Panama/Philippines arrangements are intended to front for foreign owners whose objective is flag preference benefits rather than creation of bona fide Filipino shipowning ventures.[4] Bearing in mind the fact that it is very difficult to prove the true ownership of Panamanian corporations, it is easy to see why this concern has arisen. The difficulty is that the impact of the regulatory reaction (if there is one) to the abuses is likely to fall on bona fide operations as much or more than on the abusers. If the regulatory reaction makes the arrangement no longer attractive, the abusers will find a way to leave the flag, whereas legitimate operations may not have this option.

The second concern has to do with recordation of the mortgage. A mortgage on a vessel registered in Panama will be duly recorded with the Panamanian authorities, but if the vessel then flies a flag other than that of Panama, the mortgage may not be recorded in the flag state. If, as seems likely, such a vessel calls at ports in the flag state, it is vulnerable to having other liens held to rank ahead of the mortgage. Bilateral treaties between the two countries, covering this subject would give considerable comfort, but such treaties are rare.

The third concern has to do with the basis on which the vessel is bareboat charter registered under a second flag. Bareboat charters usually have expiry dates, and one would like to be clear as to whether at the expiry date the vessel automatically reverts to the flag of convenience, or whether some specific action must be taken to cause reversion. Will a default under the bareboat charter cause automatic reversion? Along the same lines, the bareboat charter arrangement may be implemented under laws or regulations providing for temporary registration. It is not always clear whether the flag of convenience mortgage protection continues during this period, or whether it is suspended.[5]

In the absence of clearly written bodies of law in both jurisdictions and bilateral agreements providing for, among other things, dual recordation of the mortgage, the dual registry concept obviously leaves a great deal to be desired.

A second, and clearly preferable when feasible, way of dealing with the legal infrastructure problem is the finance lease. Since the financing institution owns the vessel, the mortgage is no longer a concern. The issue becomes the law and procedures for registration of title in the flag country. Most developing countries are better equipped to handle this issue than the acceptability of mortgage question. A greater obstacle than clarity of title is apt to be regulations limiting foreign investment. However, it should be possible to structure the lease with a purchase option/obligation and other terms such that the authorities can take comfort that the shipowner controls the asset in all material respects as long as the lease is not in default. Obtaining governmental acceptance of this concept may, however, require a major educational effort.

One of the major keys to a developing country shipowner's being bankable even when his country is not is the lender's or lessor's (as the case may be) claim on an internationally saleable asset. A lender's/lessor's willingness to rely on this claim depends on its degree of confidence that it will in fact be able to quickly and easily realize the value of that asset. In other words, the degree to which the financier is comfortable with its ability to quickly de-register the vessel from the flag country so that it can be sold internationally is an absolutely critical factor in making the shipowner bankable even when his country is not. This moves the discussion back into flag regulation issues. Unfortunately, neither dual registry nor finance leases addresses these issues.

The relevant flag regulations, of course, vary extensively from country to country, and the details are beyond the scope of this book. However, if the flag regulations, with particular emphasis on the de-registration question are not acceptable, the shipowner should seriously consider operating under a reputable flag of convenience.[6] This will protect the lender, but equally importantly will give the owner the flexibility to adjust the composition of its fleet from time to time in order to accommodate changing economic conditions and trading patterns. Parenthetically, unless foreign investment regulations in the flag country are especially favorable,[7] operating under a flag of convenience is likely to enhance the owner's ability to raise equity capital from international institutional investors (as distinguished from other shipowners).[8]

The decision to operate completely or partially under a flag of convenience may be politically sensitive in more than one way. For one thing, a populist regime may characterize the decision as unpatriotic. The logical answer is that otherwise, fleet growth will be limited or impossible, but in politics, the prevalence of logic is the exception rather than the rule. For another thing, foreign exchange controls may severely constrain an owner's ability to invest outside its own country.[9] If it considers investing in assets held outside the flag country, then confidentiality may be an issue, and access to the public market may be foreclosed.

Flag of convenience operations may also be politically sensitive in that the reputations of the flag of convenience registries are sometimes controversial. Certainly some registries have a better reputation than others, and there is certainly no excuse for choosing a disreputable registry. It is the nature of things today, though, that a flag of convenience shipowning group operating good tonnage managed to a high standard, can live on its own reputation rather than that of the registry. The same cannot be said for many "genuine link" registries, whether in developed or developing countries.

Lastly, it may be argued that a flag of convenience operator takes some degree of political risk on the flag country. In practice, this risk is very limited. Since it is the nature of flag of convenience operations that virtually all the operating assets are held outside the flag country, the flag country government has little leverage to force a shipowner to comply with any governmental decree or order. In theory, the greatest threat would be an attempt to nationalize the fleet, but as a practical matter, such threats are ludicrous, as there is no logical use to which such large fleets could be put by the flag government. The freedom to de-register is a major protection in law, but if one is still truly concerned, one can choose a registry whose management is known to be willing to cooperate in the de-registration process, and/or set up contingency re-registration plans with another registry known to be willing to re-register even without de-registration from the first flag.[10]

In sum, if a shipowner from a developing country operates tonnage meeting international standards; manages that tonnage to professional standards; and develops employment that does not rely exclusively on its home country market, it will be a long way to ensuring that it will be bankable whether or not its home country is bankable. One further step will be required: that of coping with home country constraints, whether they be questions of legal infrastructure, flag regulation or foreign exchange controls. This may involve attempting to change the infrastructure; using innovative schemes to live within the infrastructure; or if necessary, moving operations all or in part to a flag of convenience. The key is for the shipowner to think of itself for business purposes as a citizen of the world rather than merely of a particular country; and if anything is lacking with respect to meeting professional standards, to seek to acquire it in the international marketplace.

Greece, though a semi-industrialized rather than a developing country, has from time to time suffered from many of the same problems that plague developing countries. It is, accordingly, a very instructive case. Greek shipowners' relationship with their home government has always been uneasy. Though most would on balance prefer to fly the Greek flag, they have successfully maintained a position whereby they are able to quickly move back and forth to/from flags of convenience in reaction to the political situation of the moment. They have successfully established their operating businesses so that they are economically independent rather than wards of the flag state, and have developed international business connections that give them an independent source of foreign exchange. Last, but not least, they have successfully achieved implementation of a mortgage law that gives foreign lenders acceptable protection without raising any national sovereignty issues. As a result, Greek shipowners have generally been able to find financing even when Greece itself was having difficulty finding it.

Notes

1. I am not very sympathetic with the popular notion that financial substance criteria for borrowers in developing countries should be less stringent than elsewhere. Undercapitalization is bad for both borrower and lender, no matter where either is domiciled. In fact, one could make a strong argument that given the higher degree of risk associated with the developing country's operating environment, the criteria should be more stringent.

2. It is worth noting that this issue is not peculiar to developing country borrowers.

3. Although for reasons outlined below, I believe that developing country shipowners may be bankable before their respective countries become bankable, inducing banks to make the necessary effort to understand this will be a difficult proposition. The shipowner may be in an ironic position. The only people in a bank that know him are apt to be the staff of local offices, while the shipping expertise usually lies in the bank's offices in New York or London. Conversely, the few banks that can be induced to take an interest may lack local offices. Clearly, it is important to try to find the right bank. I believe that this is a situation that justifies employing a reputable intermediary.

4. The situation is complicated by the fact that the Philippines is a major supplier of seagoing labor to the international flag of convenience fleet. The grounds for suspicion become particularly strong when the bareboat charterer is in some way affiliated with a crewing agent.

5. This issue came to my attention when considering a proposal for Liberian registration, with bareboat charter to a Saudi Arabian company. There was no bilateral treaty. While it seemed clear that Saudi regulations permitted temporary registration on a bareboat charter basis, it was not at all clear what would happen if there were a default under the charter. I came to the conclusion that the Saudis themselves had not really considered the question, which made me fear that regardless of the wording of the law, de-registration from the Saudi flag upon occurrence of an event of default under the charter would be politically, extremely difficult to accomplish.

6. This comment is, of course, applicable to any flag not just the flags of developing countries.

7. The political environment that produces highly restrictive flag regulations is also likely to produce highly restrictive foreign investment regulations. Hence, it is unlikely that one would find the former without the latter.

8. I have deliberately not focussed in this book on the raising of equity capital from institutional investors as this market is not yet very well developed. However, the capital requirements of the industry over the next decade make it inevitable that more and more owners will seek access to the public market. There is precedent for flag of convenience and/or mixed flag of convenience/domestic flag operations' going public (Stolt Tankers, Gotaas Larsen, and Carnival Cruises, for example), and this is by and large a good thing. Apart from providing the necessary equity, it forces these companies to adhere to the financial reporting requirements of the U.S. Securities and Exchange Commission, or other applicable regulatory agencies. Such professional financial reporting is devoutly to be wished from private groups as well, regardless of nationality.

9. In my experience, people from developing countries wishing to be taken seriously as shipowners almost always have assets outside their countries. If they are serious, they should be prepared to invest at least a portion of such assets.

10. I am aware of more than one Liberian flag operator that when Sergeant Do assumed power in Monrovia, set up all the necessary corporate structure and other arrangements to re-register its entire fleet in Panama literally overnight. Likewise, I am aware of a major publicly traded cruise vessel operator that when it became concerned about the political situation in its chosen flag country, set up rather elaborate contingency plans for re-registry under another flag of convenience. Needless to say, this necessitated the cooperation of the latter.

Chapter Ten

Workouts

Most workouts occur during cyclical downturns in the market sectors the shipowner is most active in. Even when the workout situation has its basis in fraud or gross mismanagement, the workout tends to develop during the downturn, as the problems are much easier to cover up during the upturn. Dealing with workouts effectively involves development of a strategy tailored to the specific circumstances, and the appropriate choice of strategy depends on where one believes one is in the cycle and what sort of tonnage is involved. It thus behooves one to understand the nature of the supply/demand cycle for the owner's market sector(s).

There are as many theories of these cycles as there are theorists, but most of them agree on certain points. The major one is that orders for new tonnage tend to be placed more in reaction to current freight rates than to anticipated freight rates. This means that the later in the cyclical upturn that one orders (or, as the case may be, acquires second hand tonnage), the higher the contract price; the higher the capital costs; the larger (other things being equal) the amounts borrowed, and the related interest and principal amortization requirements; and the closer one is to the cyclical downturn, with its related drop in freight rates. The greatest risk for both owner and lender is at the peak of the cycle as an owner purchasing at this point will have high capital costs relative to its competition, but be facing, in the absence of previously committed employment, a declining freight rate environment. Conversely, the least risk for both is at the bottom of the cycle for exactly the opposite reasons.

This is clearly a gross oversimplication of what actually happens, but if one disaggregates the relevant markets sufficiently[1] it is still a useful approximation. The basic point is that the freight rate market reacts quickly to changes in demand for tonnage but only with a significant lag (because of the lead time required for new vessel construction) to changes in the supply. Other factors, such as changes in trading patterns, or changes in port characteristics may affect demand in the short run, but the supply constraint will continue to be an obstacle.

Clearly, unmitigated success in this business requires expert crystal ball gazing. As a practical matter, there will always be a degree of uncertainty about where one is in the cycle, but by tracking market trends; and by diversifying its portfolio of charters across time, markets, and types of tonnage, an owner can minimize the risks. However, it is unlikely that the herd instinct with respect to ordering (or not ordering, for that matter) will be superseded in the foreseeable future. Unfortunately, the second hand market is affected as well. Though the second hand buyer does not face the risk posed by the construction period, it does face the same downside risk when buying at the cyclical peak in reaction to high freight rates.

The foregoing comments apply primarily to the bulk shipping markets. The liner sector has traditionally faced some of the same syndrome, but as its underlying markets are generally less volatile, the impact has been rather less great. The focus on multiship services to specific ports known in advance, as distinct from broad worldwide market prospects for a specific vessel, may partially counteract the tendency to excess.

Most modern, fuel efficient vessels, even if only indifferently managed, are, absent fraud, able to earn sufficient revenue to cover operating costs, even in a deeply depressed market.[2] It follows that an owner that uses no debt to finance its ship purchases, preferring instead to pay cash, should not experience cash flow difficulties unless it is paying discretionary dividends to its shareholders. Thus, the amounts and terms of debt financing are critical to understanding why an owner experiences financial difficulties.

With this digression on cycles as background, one can begin to visualize the variety of scenarios that could occur, and the universe of possible solutions.

The easiest to dispose of is fraud. If there is fraud, there can no longer be a cooperative relationship between lender and owner. Any lender that believes it can control an owner/manager already known to be guilty of fraud, is indulging in gross self-delusion. This may seem obvious, but is surprisingly often ignored. The only action a lender can take is to move quickly to obtain control of the mortgaged vessels. This usually means arrest/foreclosure, but in certain instances may be achieved by the exercise of rights under a pledge of shares.

If, on the other hand, management is incompetent but not dishonest,[3] a lender has at least a little more flexibility. Its basic objective must be to install competent management. This sounds simple until one considers that the incumbent management is not likely to be cooperative. Because of the "lender liability" issue (see note 23 to Chapter Eight), one must be very careful about how this is handled. The ideal, of course, would be for the shareholders to take some action on their own initiative, or with only gentle prodding, but as a practical matter, management and shareholders are usually the same, or at least overlap considerably. It may come down to obtaining control of the vessels by arrest/foreclosure, followed by installation of new management chosen by the lender.

If the operating management is competent, but financial results have not been adequate for debt service because of market downturns, errors with respect to types of vessels purchased or the timing of vessel purchases, or some combination thereof, there may be room for a cooperative arrangement between lender and borrower. If the owner is able to pay interest and the type of tonnage involved is modern and/or otherwise has good long term prospects, it may be possible to justify deferral of principal payments even though the finance ratio, because of depreciation of vessel values, has risen above 100%. If the rest of the owner's fleet, on the basis of depreciated vessel values, is underleveraged, it may be possible to cross collateralize, thus improving the security position as an inducement to lender patience.

Most lenders will not and probably should not be patient with respect to interest payments. The "rolling up" of interest payments and adding them to the amount of the loan is a rather dangerous practice, as the finance ratio can very quickly become wildly out of control. A reduced rate of interest may on rare occasions make sense, but only if the lender is highly confident about the long range future of the tonnage. A lender agreeing to a reduced interest loan has agreed to impair the value of the loan, and will probably be required by its auditors and/or its regulatory authorities to write it down. Therefore, it will most likely demand a quid pro quo of some sort, probably a shareholding in the owning company, or an interest in the residual value of the vessel.[4] The realizeable values of such quid quo pros are problematic at best, however, and a lender should be extremely careful when considering this option. In a few cases, it may be possible to reduce debt by sale of assets, allowing the owner to continue in business on a smaller scale.

If the owner is unable to pay the interest due, and/or the vessel is old enough or of a type to have questionable long range prospects, the vessel should probably be sold or scrapped, preferably quickly before the sale and purchase and/or scrap markets deteriorate further. If both parties are realistic, this can be done by mutual agreement. Historically, however, lenders go into a minor state of shock upon understanding that the realizeable value of the vessel is less than the amount of the loan,[5] and that consequently they will be forced to write-off at least a portion of it. On the other hand, owners, probably quicker than lenders to recognize the likely shortfall, suddenly realize that the likelihood of the lenders' calling any corporate and/or personal guarantees outstanding will rise dramatically, and discover many reasons to defer the sale. This is a situation to be avoided, as it often leads to no action at all, and may be as dangerous as indulging in wishful thinking about the long term prospects for the vessels. It is better for both parties to recognize the loss early on before it grows as a result of unpaid interest, and results in a larger claim under the guarantees. If it is not possible to accomplish this by mutual agreement, it may be necessary for a lender to once again consider the arrest/foreclosure option.

The common thread in each of these three scenarios is at least the possibility of arrest/foreclosure. This process is full of surprises for the unsuspecting lender. The first surprise is that the rules and procedures vary widely depending on where the vessel is arrested. The details of these are beyond the scope of this book, but a good litigator from a law firm with an established admiralty practice should have this information.[6] With this information available, and knowing the vessel's voyage route,[7] one can proceed to attempt to choose an arresting port at which the rules and procedures are the most favorable or at least the least unfavorable. There is significant risk involved in this, however. The mortgagee is not the only party that can arrest the ship. If suppliers or other unsecured creditors choose to arrest the vessel at an intervening port, there is little that the mortgagee can do other than to see that its rights are protected according to the rules prevailing in that port.

The second surprise, is that the mortgagee, despite being a secured creditor (and very likely the only secured creditor) is never the first priority claimant. Court and arrest costs almost always rank first. Usually the mortgage explicitly recognizes the higher priority of salvage claims, crew wages, and perhaps cash advances to the vessel by its master. Not recognized are in rem (as distinguished from in persona) claims, or claims against the vessel as distinguished from claims against its owner. The in rem doctrine in admiralty is a very old concept resulting from the fact that as a vessel moved around the world, it required various services in local ports. In the absence of electronic communications, it was possible to communicate in advance with the owner only if he was on board. The in rem concept arose as a way of protecting the local suppliers of services, such as stevedoring, victualling, chandlery, and fuel. How the in rem claims rank with respect to the mortgage varies widely from country to country, from port to port within a country, and/or even from case to case within a port depending on the sophistication, political sensitivity, and/or corruptibility of the legal system involved. The amounts can be substantial, particularly if suppliers of bunkers are held to have a higher priority claim.

To complicate the issue even further, a multi-vessel owner is unlikely to experience financial difficulties with one vessel without also experiencing them with others. Consequently, there are frequently efforts to arrest a vessel for claims actually pertaining to another vessel under common ownership under the so-called sister ship concept.[8] On the face of it, such an effort takes the claim out of in rem status into in persona status, but courts and statutes in various jurisdictions differ greatly in their handling of it.

The third surprise is that, adding insult to injury, the mortgagee may now have to lay out some additional funds.

First, the arresting law enforcement authority will wish to be paid. Second, the court of jurisdiction may require posting of a bond to cover its costs. Third, the crew will need to be provided for. This means that any wages owed will have to be paid, and provision for repatriation made.[9] Last, but not necessarily least, the needs of the ship will have to be provided for. This means arranging for berthing, skeleton crew, supplies, and insurance. While it is true that all these outlays are recoverable under any properly drafted mortgage, they will reduce the spread between the market value of the vessel and the amount of the loan or (as the case may be) increase the amount of the loss.

The fourth surprise is the low ''fire sale'' values achievable upon sale of the vessel. Most arresting jurisdictions provide for some form of auction procedure. Prospective buyers, because of a vessel's poor condition (likely to be the case if its previous owner was financially weak) or of fears that any remaining in rem claims will continue to plague the vessel's future operations,[10] are often unwilling to contemplate a bid at the then prevailing ''willing buyer, willing seller'' market value, and the court may well set time constraints on a proper sales effort. This predicament often induces the lender, which usually has the most to lose, to buy the vessel itself on the theory that a more orderly sale at a time and under conditions of its choosing, is likely to achieve a better price.[11]

At this juncture, assuming that the lender now owns the vessel, it must make a series of decisions. Should it promptly re-sell or scrap the vessel, or hold it in hopes of a market turnaround?[12] If it decides to hold it, should it lay it up, or attempt to trade it? If the latter, how shall it arrange for the chartering and management of the vessel?

The answers to the first two questions depend on where one is in the supply/demand cycle for the vessel in question and the vessel's age. For example, if the cycle is at or near the beginning of the downturn, it appears that the adjustment period will be long, and the vessel is in the latter stages of its useful life, it probably makes sense to sell it promptly, or in an extreme case, scrap it. In contrast, if it is a relatively modern vessel at the same cyclical stage, it may make sense to hold it for resale in an improved market. However, the analysis should be rigorous, as in theory, unless the present value of the expected value appreciation exceeds the carrying costs (including interest on funding) net of any income from trading the vessel, the decision will not make economic sense. Obviously, the required appreciation can be considerable if the elapsed time to turnaround is long and one uses an appropriately high discount rate to reflect the high level of uncertainty with respect to the validity of the assumptions.[13] Likewise, the decision to layup or trade the vessel depends on whether the freight rates that can be earned on an extended basis will cover not only the vessel's operating costs, but also the costs of activation from layup (if necessary), and still make at least a contribution to the financial carrying costs.

All this sounds rather technical perhaps. Despite the uncertainties surrounding the assumptions, though, the attempt to quantify the problem can at least identify the issues critical to success, and the minimum conditions necessary to make any given decision work. The availability of personal computers makes the design of a model for this analysis rather simple, and what-if analysis will result in better informed judgmental decisions.

If a lender decides to hold the vessel pending future sale and purchase market improvement, it must decide how to provide for chartering and management decisions. Few lending institutions are equipped to handle these internally with a satisfactory degree of competence, and therefore they must arrange for outside assistance. Usually, they are best served by contracting with a professional, independent ship management company, but should be careful to appoint one with no conflicts of interest. A lender may be tempted to look to its other, still solvent clients for assistance,[14] and in depressed times, these clients are often grateful for the opportunity to supplement their vessel revenues with management fees. However, unless their business involves the same type of vessel as the one to be managed, their level of competence is questionable. On the other hand, if their business involves the same type of vessel, they have an inherent conflict of interest. Consequently, such an arrangement with clients is seldom a good idea.

All this is bad enough if there is only one lender. If there are multiple lenders participating in a syndicate, the syndicate will have one of the lenders act as agent. There are several issues that arise here. First, in most syndications, the agent will control the documentation process. A participant can forestall many problems for itself by carefully reviewing the documentation before participating, and bowing out of it would have to make too many compromises. Poorly drafted documentation, if the transaction becomes a workout, makes it necessary to litigate questions that need not otherwise be litigated, and may result in unnecessary losses. This is in nobody's best interest. A participant's documentation review should give special attention to the terms of the participation agreement. In today's banking market, in which banks make a business of buying and selling loans, participation agreements often limit a participant's rights to approval of any changes of terms of repayment, or changes in interest rates (sometimes even these changes can be approved by a majority vote of the participants). Also, some bank syndications departments, being unfamiliar with the nature of ship financings, try to use "boiler plate" participation agreements that do not recognize the essential nature of the transaction as secured.

With all these difficulties, it is clearly preferable to be an assignee rather than a participant. A participant merely buys an interest in a loan made by someone else, whereas an assignee becomes a direct party to the loan agreement, and has all the rights of the original lender as well as a pari passu interest in the security package. Among other things, the agent's responsibilities are defined either in the loan agreement or in a separate agency agreement, and hence there is a standard to which it can be held. This becomes particularly relevant if the loan becomes a workout.

A second issue is that an agent bank may be subject to a conflict of interest if it has business relationships with the owner above and beyond the one for which it is agent. On the one hand, it may wish to protect its non-lending business relationship, and consequently not act as aggressively as it should. On the other hand, to generate cash to reduce other debts it may act to sell vessels sooner than it should. Either way, it will be its own interests that are being served, not necessarily the best interests of the syndicate.[15]

A third issue is that banks vary quite widely in their reputations for integrity and competence when acting as agents. This really becomes important during workout situations, as the workouts may present the greatest temptations to abuse. Furthermore, different banks handle workouts in different ways (and shipping workouts sometimes in special ways within their workout responsibilities), and it definitely pays to know and assess the people in that position. Clearly, one would not wish to end up with a workout being handled by a bank's general syndications or loan sales department.

Being aware of all these problems, many experienced ship financing banks refuse as a matter of policy to be involved in syndicated ship financings.

In a syndicated loan, the borrower deals only with the agent, just as if there were only one lender. When an owner has multiple lenders and/or syndicates/agents, the workout becomes much more complex. The lenders may have different levels of competence and expertise; have more or less attention from their managements; the personalities and egos of the people involved may clash; and most importantly, their interests may differ. As one example only, some may have stronger security positions than others, or may be involved with tonnage with better prospects. The differences would logically lead to different courses of action. However, often the largest or lead lender will attempt to stampede or induce the others into a course of action serving its best interests rather than theirs (egos often come into play here). A small lender should not be intimidated or overly impressed, as its judgment is apt to be just as good or better than that of its larger colleagues. It should make decisions and take actions in its own best interests, whether or not these are the same as those of the lead.

Most of this chapter has been written from the point of view of the lender, as in a workout situation, the lender tends to be "in the driver's seat." Once it is in default, the owner has an extremely weak bargaining position. There are, however, a few things it can do to make the impact of the workout less devastating.

First, at the first sign of potential problems, it should arrange for the assistance of expert legal counsel.

Second, and perhaps most critical, it should open communications with the lender(s) at the first sign of difficulties. Usually severe cash flow difficulties do not occur without warning, and if the owner waits to communicate the difficulties until after default, it risks a panicked reaction from the lender(s). This is to be avoided at all costs, as the calling of one loan, together with related actions to arrest ships, can very easily, by way of cross default provisions trigger actions against other vessels, bank accounts, etc. Operations can come very quickly to a halt, often totally unnecessarily. Obviously, such a situation is in the interests of neither borrower nor lender. Experienced shipping lenders will already be aware of the market conditions that could result in problems, but it is inadvisable to rely on this. Lenders vary widely in their degree of competence and experience.

Third, it should adopt a policy of totally open communications with its lenders. It should promptly, honestly, and completely comply with all requests for information, even if they appear unnecessary or irrelevant. Its senior management should always be available on short notice to meet with or converse with the lender(s).

Fourth, it should not automatically protest at the idea of disposing of vessels.

Voluntary reduction of the scale of operations will result in a greater likelihood of remaining in business for the long run, and will yield better values for the assets than would be obtainable by forcing the lender(s) into an arrest/foreclosure mode. Instead of protesting, it should attempt to influence the lender(s) to dispose of those vessels earning the lowest current returns and having the worst long term prospects. Reference to the supply/demand cycle concept for its vessels may be helpful here, although a receptive ear on the lender's side cannot be guaranteed.

Fifth, the owner should at least consider the possibility of appointing an intermediary to represent it to all the lenders. This is particularly to be recommended when there are multiple lenders, as a competent intermediary can often succeed in standardizing the information requests. It can also defuse the impact of personal emotions, as these often run rather high on both sides in workout situations. However, the intermediary should be chosen carefully. He, she, or it should have a relationship of trust with the owner, and should enjoy an independent reputation for fairness and competence. Likewise, and perhaps most importantly, the intermediary should "speak both languages"; i.e. have a knowledge of both the shipping industry and the finance business. The most effective people of this sort tend to be ex-shipping bankers.[16]

The discussion in this chapter demonstrates conclusively that workouts are never happy situations for either borrower or lender. At the very least they cause heartache, while at worst they result in massive losses to both sides. It is to be hoped that the prescriptions and analytical techniques outlined in this book will make such situations increasingly rare, and ameliorate the impact of those that do occur.

Notes

1. Considering, for example, products tankers in the 50,000-80,000 DWT range, rather than the tanker market taken as a whole.

2. If this is not true, the vessel should probably be scrapped.

3. In practice it is very hard to tell the difference.

4. There are a number of former owners now in business strictly as vessel managers for their own former vessels, now owned by commercial banks.

5. The purpose of security maintenance clauses is the preservation of an acceptable finance ratio, but even if the borrower lacks other resources with which to "top up" the security package, it still serves a useful purpose in alerting a lender to unfavorable developments. The hope is that the vessel can be sold before the deteriorating sale and purchase market causes the finance ratio to rise to or above 100%. In practice, this can only work if the lender is willing and able to act quickly on the information. Without management cooperation, the necessity to arrest/foreclose may result in loss-widening delays.

6. Any lender attempting arrest/foreclosure without this kind of assistance is setting itself up for a grossly sub-optimal result. When a workout situation has become this confrontational, the various parties, which include other creditors and their legal counsel, will inevitably try to manipulate the procedures and negotiations to their own best advantage. Consequently, it is well to have a litigator with an earned reputation for toughness and even unpleasantness.

7. If this information cannot be obtained from management, information provided by management is deemed unreliable, or for whatever reason the lender does not wish to alert management to the possibility of arrest, there are a number of independent services that make a business out of tracking vessel movements.

8. A workout situation I once participated in involved a vessel that was originally arrested by the major oil company that was its principal supplier of bunkers. We were at first appalled by the size of the claim until we realized that it represented the total claim against the owner's fleet of over forty vessels rather than just the claim against the ship over which we held a mortgage. The difference was in multiple seven figures, and considerable litigation resulted, although in this case, the court held that the bunker claim was junior to the mortgage.

9. It is well to move quickly on this matter. Apart from ethical niceties, an unpaid crew with little work to do, on a vessel possibly running low on victuals, in a port far from home, can create an explosive situation. I have never been unfortunate enough to have to negotiate with such a crew, but former colleagues tell stories of being implicitly or explicitly threatened with physical violence. Likewise, the plight of a stranded crew can easily become a political cause celebre in the port city. Rightly or wrongly, the mortgagee is often perceived as the cause of the crew's plight, and this can unfavorably affect the litigation of the claim.

10. Theoretically, once the auction procedure and distribution of the proceeds has been completed, these claims should be extinguished. However, as a practical matter, these creditors may attempt to arrest the vessel at ensuing ports of call under new ownership. At best, the new owner will have to litigate to defend itself against the claims, but at worst, a court in another jurisdiction may give priority to claims not given priority by the original court. In the latter case, the new owner will have to pay the claim, or lose the vessel by legal proceedings. Prospective buyers tend to discount their bids to reflect these factors.

11. As an example of an "exception that proves the rule," the one vessel auction that ever involved me (albeit indirectly) resulted in sale to a major Japanese trading company at a price in excess of what the failed owner had paid for it. This circumstance was attributable to the facts that this specific type and size of vessel actually appreciated in value at a time that most ship values were depreciating, and that it exactly matched certain of the buyer's special requirements. As a result, the lender came out whole. Obviously luck was a factor here, but attention to the business cycle for this type of vessel also played a part. I had only agreed to the financing because I could see from the purchase price contracted and other market information that this type of vessel was at or close to its cyclical trough, and that the upside potential was much greater than the downside risk. In fact, the owner's financial difficulties were not attributable to this vessel, but to other vessels in its fleet.

12. The decision to hold it can result in some amusing accounting issues. One of my previous employers, as the result of a bankruptcy, became the owner of a somewhat elderly tanker, and decided to hold it. When the auditors first examined the bank's books, they could not find it. They later found it under the heading "furniture and equipment." A bank's accounting procedures are obviously not well suited to ship ownership. After much cogitation, the auditors forced the bank to re-classify the vessel under the heading "other assets."

13. A lender deciding to hold a vessel may be able to take advantage of the tax benefits of ownership, mainly depreciation. If so, the tax effect can be factored into the analysis.

14. I am informed of at least one major money center bank that went so far as to sell a number of vessels it had come into possession of, to one of its major clients at prices reflecting the amounts outstanding under the original loans; i.e. at artificially inflated prices. It then provided 100% financing on accommodating terms, and indemnified the buyer against depreciation in the market value of the vessels. The obvious purpose was to avoid having to recognize the losses on the original loans, and is consequently a self-delusionary and hence dangerous practice. It may even be illegal, but at the very least does not meet sound audit standards. In fact, it can work only if the new owner can, on an extended basis, earn enough from operating the vessels to pay interest and principal on a very heavy debt load. Given the now prevailing dry cargo market, this is unlikely at best. Auditors will eventually question why the 100% financing is not being repaid, and then the scheme will come unraveled, and the people responsible, if they are still there, will be appropriately disciplined.

15. Participating banks should be very wary of relying for protection on old, established business relationships with other banks, or on a historical reputation for competence and fair dealing. In my experience, workouts bring out the worst in interbank relationships. When facing a possible loss, even the best of them will look after their own interests first.

16. I always felt that the appointment of Shearson Lehman Brothers to represent the C.Y. Tung Group when it was experiencing financial difficulties was a mistake. Though this firm enjoys an excellent reputation as an investment house, it has little knowledge of the shipping industry. It is interesting that Shearson implicitly recognized this fact by obtaining the assistance of one of the professional intermediaries mentioned in Chapter Six.

Appendix A

Types of Vessel, Modes of Operation, Types of Employment

There are various ways the shipping markets can be broken-up for analytical purposes. One useful way is to break them into five groups: liquid cargo, dry bulk, liner, offshore, and specialized.

Liquid cargo operations are typified by the well-known tanker concept. Tankers come in many shapes and sizes from a few hundred deadweight tons to well over half-a-million deadweight tons. What is less well-known is that there are a number of different types of tankers with different levels of technological sophistication depending on the nature of the cargoes to be carried. Most (including all of the biggest ones) have no special pumping systems or tank coatings, and are designed only for crude oil. Products tankers, on the other hand, have special pumping systems to allow carriage of several segregated products. In addition, they usually have tanks especially coated with epoxy, and heating coils in the tanks. These allow them to carry so-called "clean," or refined, petroleum products.

While the distinction between products tankers and chemical or parcel tankers is sometimes a fine one, generally the parcel tankers are equipped to carry a greater variety (up to fifty) of segregated products. Thus, they have even more sophisticated pumping systems, as well as rather sophisticated tank cleaning equipment. In addition, as they are designed to be able to carry such corrosive products as phosphoric acid, at least some of their tanks are usually lined with stainless steel or zinc.

Liquified gas tankers represent perhaps the ultimate in technological sophistication, as these vessels must be constructed so as to maintain the cargo at extremely low temperatures and/or under high pressure.

Lastly, there are a number of specialized tankers, each with its own special characteristics. Latex, asphalt, and alcoholic beverage carriers are good examples.

The dry bulk market refers to the transportation of dry cargo in bulk: that is to say, in ship-load lots. Typical cargoes include iron ore, coal, grain, bauxite, phosphate rock, and sugar. The typical vessel is the bulkcarrier. Bulkcarriers differ from one another primarily in terms of size (which may range from roughly 10,000dwt to 250,000dwt) and gearing. Gearing refers to the amount, type, and size of loading and unloading equipment (cranes, gantries, etc.) carried on board the vessel. Gear adds flexibility, as this equipment can enable the vessel to call at ports that lack suitable unloading equipment. Dry bulk cargoes of less than 10,000 tons are usually carried in singledeckers (really just small bulkcarriers) or so-called tweendeckers, which have a middle deck dividing the holds. This makes it possible to carry a variety of part cargoes, but tween deckers are nevertheless commonly used to carry small bulk cargoes.

Form of employment plays an important role in the analysis of financings for tankers and bulkcarriers. Tramping refers to the situation that exists when a vessel is chartered to a shipper for no longer than a single voyage. This is often referred to as the spot market. Sometimes tramp operators benefit from so-called contracts of affreightment (COA's) in which a shipper theoretically guarantees a certain volume of cargo over a specified period of time at a specified freight rate. Unfortunately, these contracts are seldom enforceable in a weak market. Spot rates are typically quoted on an all-in basis, including bunker (fuel) and port costs. COA's are typically quoted in dollars per ton, though extended term COA's often include clauses providing for rate adjustments if bunker and port costs increase. Last is the time or period charter, in which the shipowner puts his vessel at the disposal of a shipper for a specified period of time. This might be as short as the length of a particular voyage, or as long as twenty-five years. Because voyages to be undertaken are not pre-determined, time charter rates are typically quoted in dollars per deadweight ton per month, or dollars per day, with the charterer responsible for all bunker and port costs.

Many shipping bankers are tempted to assume that the time charter, because it seemingly guarantees a revenue stream, is the only bankable form of employment. This is a mistake, as the time charter obscures certain definite traps. First, it ignores the fact that the charter is worth no more than the charterer. Second, it tempts one to ignore the shipowner's obligation to perform. If he does not perform, charterhire will not be paid, and therefore the time charter loses its value as security. Third, unless it provides for escalation, the owner may be caught by inflating operating costs in later years. Lastly, the state of the market becomes an important factor: it makes no economic sense to either the owner or the bank to sign a long-term time charter when the market is depressed. The point to all this is that the reputation of the owner and his ability to perform are more important than the specific form of employment.

These forms of employment are especially typical of the liquid cargo and dry bulk markets. To a lesser degree they also apply to the offshore and specialized sectors. However, the liner sector is fundamentally different.

Cargo liner services are based on the concept of a group of ships maintaining a specified schedule of calls among a specified series of ports, loading and unloading cargoes (rarely in ship-load lots) at each port. A liner service may use either owned or chartered vessels, or a combination of the two, and the freights earned are really the earnings of the line, rather than of a specific vessel. Analysis of this type of credit is much closer to conventional balance sheet/income statement analysis than is the case with bulk shipping business.

The basic type of ship for a breakbulk liner service, in which there is no predetermined form or method to the loading procedure, is the general cargo vessel. Generally speaking, the general cargo vessel is a geared version of the tweendecker. In the last fifteen years or so, however, the growth of the container ship, which allows a vessel, by using unitized cargoes, to load and unload much more efficiently, has brought the container ship to prominence. The capacity of these ships is usually measured in TEU, or twenty-foot equivalent units (i.e., the number of twenty-foot containers, or the equivalent capacity in forty-foot containers). Container vessels have been built in sizes ranging from 200TEU to 4,148TEU, these last being the series constructed in Korea for U.S. Lines.

Lastly, lines often use ro/ro or roll-on/roll-off ships. These are frequently employed in liner services where there is a lot of wheeled cargo, usually trailers. These ships carry large stern or side ramps that make it easy to load or unload wheeled cargo without any sophisticated port equipment.

In recent years there has been increasing pressure on the lines to provide a door-to-door transportation service. To this end, many of the lines have now combined in one manner or another with trucking companies and/or railroads to offer so-called intermodal services.

Offshore oil and gas exploration has resulted in the development of certain shipping related requirements. The most obvious are drilling rigs, accommodation platforms, offshore supply vessels to service the rigs, and various types of diving, pipelaying, and fire-fighting vessels. Despite the fact that these "vessels" are employed in providing a service rather than in cargo transportation, they are legally registered and documented as marine transportation equipment and, therefore, are subject to similar finance arrangements.

Specialized vessels include tug/barge, towing, anchor-handling, and heavy lift. These are self-explanatory. There are, however, two other special ships worthy of mention. The reefer is a refrigerated vessel designed primarily for carrying fresh fruit and frozen meat. As the importing countries are rarely fruit or meat exporters, the return voyages are usually based on general cargo and automobiles. Pure car carriers, on the other hand, are designed to handle the volume of international trade in automobiles. They are usually operated under contracts of affreightment from Japan to the U.S. or Europe.

Appendix B

Materials to be Presented to Lenders

Incomplete information packages create nothing but frustration for both prospective lender and prospective borrower; the former because it does not believe the borrower understands its needs, and hence creates much unnecessary work; and the latter because the extra work results in delays, which the borrower interprets as lack of responsiveness. What follows is intended to be a rough guide to what information will normally be required, but given that each transaction is unique, one should approach the problem with common sense.

Figure 7 is a list of typically required information. Some items are necessary only in the context of a new relationship, and need only be updated in the context of an ongoing relationship. A prospective borrower or lender may wish to convert this list into some variation of a checklist.

The background memorandum is very important, but need not be excessively long. It should give some history of the company or group, outline its corporate structure and ownership, explain its business strategy both present and future, and list the management team with relevant details of its background (age, education, experience, etc.). Last, but not least, it should outline any matters of business or operating philosophy that are particularly important to the borrower.

Figure 7

List of Typically Required Information

1. Transaction as proposed by the borrower.

2. Background memorandum.

3. Full details of vessel(s) to be financed, with shipbroker valuations (optional).

4. Borrower's audited financial statements for preceding five years, and most recent unaudited quarterly statement.

5. Corporate guarantor's audited financial statements for preceding five years and most recent unaudited quarterly statement.

6. Personal guarantor's personal financial statement.

7. Fleet list, including employment details.

8. Cash flow forecast, including detailed assumptions, for the vessel(s) to be financed.

9. Fleet cash flow forecast, including detailed assumptions.

10. Copies of time charters (if any) relating to the vessel(s) to be financed.

11. Copies of construction contracts if the financing relates to newbuildings.

12. References (bankers, brokers, charterers, suppliers, agents, etc.), including name, address and telephone number of primary contact.

Vessel details (also applies to fleet list) should include the name of the vessel; shipyard at which constructed, and date of delivery; type of vessel; size in gross registered tons, deadweight tons (or other relevant measure of cargo capacity: cubic feet for reefers and gas carriers, or twenty foot equivalent units for container ships, for instance), and light-weight tons (relevant for calculation of scrap value); gearing if any; employment details (i.e. spot or time charter, with name of charterer, freight rate, term of charter, and expiry date); and name of managing agent. It does no harm (and may do some good) to include shipbroker valuations, but the lender should still obtain its own independent valuations.

Most lenders have a standard form for personal financial statements, and borrowers should use it. The statements should be prepared on a basis that excludes the person's interests in shipowning ventures.

It is very helpful to a lender if these materials are presented in a logical order, and in a neat package. Cosmetics are important; a sloppy or incomplete information package can deter a lender from what may otherwise be an outstanding business transaction. The cost of preparing a clean and neat package is only a token compared to the potential return on the transaction to both borrower and lender.

Appendix C

Sample Commitment Letter

LETTERHEAD

January 00, 1988

____
____
____
New York, New York 10017

Gentlemen/Mesdames:

We are pleased to advise you that subject to the terms and conditions outlined below, the______________________________________Bank, acting through its Grand Cayman Branch, is willing to make available to you the loan facility outlined below:

A AMOUNT: Up to a maximum of U.S. $5,000,000.

B PURPOSE: To finance a portion of the purchase price of the motor tanker presently named ____________, of ________deadweight tons, built at the ________shipyard in Japan in 19____, and presently registered under the flag of the Republic of Singapore.

C TERM: 4 years.

D DRAWDOWN: Upon three business days written notice following completion of documentation.

E REPAYMENT: Fifteen quarterly instalments of $250,000 each; followed by one instalment of $1,250,000.

F INTEREST: The loan will bear interest calculated at LIBOR (the rate at which the ________________Bank, London, offers to place deposits of similar amount and duration with prime Eurodollar banks), plus a spread of 1-½% per annum. Interest will be calculated on the basis of the actual days elapsed and a 360 day year, and will be payable quarterly in arrears.

G FACILITY FEE: $25,000 payable at drawdown.

H COMMITMENT FEE: ½% per annum on the amount committed, but not yet drawn. The fee will be calculated on the basis of the actual days elapsed between the date of your acceptance of this commitment and the drawdown date, and a 360 day year, and will be payable at drawdown.

I SECURITY:

1. First Preferred Liberian Mortgage over the M/T
We understand that the vessel will be re-registered in the Republic of Liberia.

2. General assignment of your earnings from shipping operations.

3. Specific assignment of a contract of affreightment dated October ____, 1987 between yourselves and ____.

4. Specific assignment of a contract of affreightment dated __________, 1988 between yourselves and __________________Corporation.

5. Specific assignment of the time charter dated ____________________, 1987 (applying to the M/T ______________) between yourselves and the ____________________________.

6. Assignment of all the vessel's insurances. Insurances must be in an amount equal to at least 130% of the total amount of the loan, and must be on terms acceptable to us. If the insurance is placed with a "captive" insurance company, all reinsurances will be assigned to us, and will be placed with underwriters acceptable to us. We will take out mortgagee's interest insurance at your expense.

7. Assignment of the vessel's management contract with

8. Several but unconditional corporate guarantees of your shareholders: ; ; and

J OTHER CONDITIONS:

1. This commitment is subject to our satisfactory examination of the contracts of affreightment and the time charter that will be assigned.

2. You will maintain a current account with the Bank, London. All charterhire and other receipts due under the assignments will be paid to or deposited in a charterhire account under our sole control. Both the current account and the charterhire account will be pledged to us. On a monthly basis, we will retain from the charterhire account: a) ⅓ of the next succeeding quarterly payment of principal and interest; and b) such additional amounts as may be required to meet the terms of J 3. below. The amounts so retained will be placed in one or more interest-bearing deposits maturing on the immediately succeeding principal and interest payment date, and the deposit(s) will be pledged to us. Upon maturity, the accumulated funds due to us will be paid to us; and amounts still required to meet the terms of J 3. will continue to be retained. Absent any event of default, any funds remaining in the charterhire account (including accumulated interest on interest-bearing deposits) will be paid to the current account, which though pledged to us, will be under your control.

3. The M/T will be subject to annual appraisals by shipbrokers acceptable to us at your expense. If at any time, on the basis of such appraisals or other appraisals arranged at our expense the value of the vessel is found to be below 140% of all amounts due under the loan agreement and all the security documents, you will either: a) provide such additional security acceptable to us as will make the total security available to us equal to or greater than 140% of such amounts due; or b) prepay amounts (such amounts to be applied in inverse order of maturity) sufficient to make the total security available to us equal to or greater than 140% of the remaining amounts due.

4. You may prepay the loan in amounts of $500,000 (or multiples thereof) on any interest payment date, provided that you give us at least 30 days written notice. Such prepayments will be applied in inverse order of their maturity.

5. This commitment letter, and all loan and security documentation, will be governed by the laws of the State of New York, with the exception of the mortgage, which will be governed by the laws of the Republic of Liberia; and for the pledges of accounts, which will be governed by the laws of England.

K DOCUMENTATION: All documentation, agreements, and legal matters in connection with this transaction shall be in form and substance satisfactory to us, and shall contain such additional terms and conditions, not conflicting herewith, as we may deem necessary or appropriate. We may also, as a condition of this loan, require the presentation of additional materials including, without limitation, such certificates, legal opinions, financial statements or other information as we may request.

By your acceptance hereof, you agree that whether or not the transaction herein contemplated is consummated, you will reimburse us for all out-of-pocket costs and expenses incurred in connection with the drafting and preparation of the documents relating to the transaction, including, without limitation, the fees and expenses of our legal counsel.

This offer will expire on February , 1988.

If the foregoing terms and conditions are acceptable to you, please sign, date, and return the enclosed photocopy of this letter.

Yours truly,

BANK

General Manager Vice President

(ON PHOTOCOPY ONLY)

ACCEPTED and AGREED:

___

by:

title:

date:

Also from Fairplay Publications:

Shipping Finance

by J E Sloggett

Alone in its field, this book is written for an "informed" maritime readership, but one which may not have a detailed knowledge of financial practices employed in the complex world of ship finance. Written by a consultant naval architect with extensive experience of financial negotiation in the purchase of both ships and offshore craft, this is first and foremost a practical handbook in which the procedures and terms are fully covered. Both new and secondhand craft are reviewed. The book details the financial appraisal of new projects while the use of foreign currency, taxation and leasing are among the important subjects described in this work.

Financial Risk Management — in the shipping industry

by James Gray

The purpose of this volume is to discuss the management of marine commercial risks, comparing traditional period time chartering, contract of affreightment against new building and joint ventures, with freight futures, which is a new method of commercial risk management. The working of freight futures markets BIFFEX and INTEX are fully explained and the author details how these markets can offer a cheap, flexible and easy to use tool. The use of the financial futures market to control currency and interest rate risk is also described.

THE FINANCING OF SHIP ACQUISITIONS

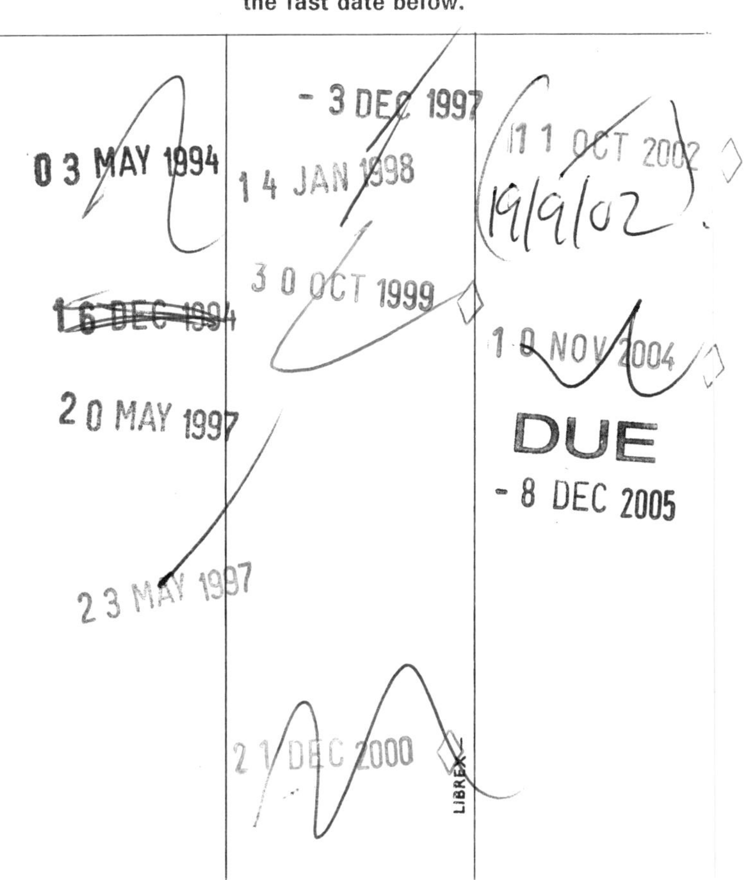